The Hulton Getty Picture Collection

DECADES OF

FASHION

D0311285

The Hulton Getty Picture Collection

DECADES OF

Harriet Worsley

KÖNEMANN

First published in 2000 by Könemann Verlagsgesellschaft mbH, Bonner Strasse 126, D-50968 Köln

This book was produced by The Hulton Getty Picture Collection Limited,
Unique House, 21–31 Woodfield Road, London W9 2BA

Art director: Michael Rand
Design: Tea McAleer
Editor: Richard Collins
Picture research: Ali Khoja, Leon Meyer
Project manager: Leon Meyer
Proof reader & indexer: Liz Ihre
Special thanks: Alex Linghorn, Antonia Hille, Tom Worsley, Jamie Knight, Sarah McDonald,
Deirdre McGale, Arlete Santos, Nancy Glowinski, Mary Welland

Colour separation by Omniascanners Srl., Milan
Printed and bound by Star Standard Industries Ltd.
Printed in Singapore

ISBN 3-8290-1280-2
10 9 8 7 6 5 4 3 2 1

Frontispiece: Sixties model Lesley Hornby, more famously known
as Twiggy, personified the girl–child ideal of the decade with her
tiny body, big eyes and crop by hairdresser Leonard. Twiggy took
the fashion industry by storm with the help of another hairdresser, Nigel John Davies, who reinvented himself as Justin de
Villeneuve. She looked good in the school uniform-style mini-
dresses designed by Mary Quant and was a household name by
the time she 'retired' at nineteen. This picture from 1967 shows
her wearing the bold, black eye make-up fashionable at the time,
complete with fake eyelashes.

Contents

Introduction

Twentieth-century fashion began in one particular city – Paris – and it was towards this city and to French designers like Charles Frederick Worth, Paul Poiret and Coco Chanel that Western women looked to direct their taste in clothes. During the Second World War, when Paris was isolated by German occupation, Britain and America found that necessity proved to be the mother of invention and they developed their own fashion styles. Post-war prosperity created a youth culture that spawned what is now called street-level or 'underground' fashion.

By the end of the century, the fashion cycle was operating on fast forward; no one trend held sway. As one silhouette evolved, another reacted to it the following season. Women now had unprecedented access to global fashion. They could choose styles from any country in the world, order clothing over the Internet or visit a distant country and buy pieces herself. By the year 2000 Paris, New York, London, Milan and Sydney were hosting high-profile fashion shows and countries such as Japan, Belgium and Holland were throwing new designers out onto the international playing field.

As attitudes towards women changed during the century, so did their clothing; the cycle of change was endless. Certain looks and silhouettes recur throughout the period. Obvious examples include curvaceous styles with heaving bosoms, narrow waists and wide skirts; the square-cut, boyish look; and the fluid, draped fabrics influenced by Ancient Greece. In 1947 *Picture Post* remarked perceptively: 'Nothing is so disliked, nothing so despised as yesterday's fashion. We invariably find our parents' taste in clothes … intolerable. But, equally certainly, a succeeding generation will discover in them nostalgic beauty and forgotten charm. Once they belong to the day before yesterday their revival is certain.' French designer Christian Lacroix offered his own analysis: 'Fashion comes round in an Oedipal cycle; a young designer is forever trying bring back to life the first female image that made an impression on him. The twenty-year-old designers of today are always nostalgic for the glamour of their childhood.'

Several threads run through 20th-century fashion. Haute couture clothing is exclusive, made-to-measure clothing fitted to the individual's exact proportions. Prêt-à-porter, in contrast, is ready-to-wear. The designer's creations are mass-produced in a range of standardised sizes. Feeding off the trends set by expensive, designer fashion are a host of businesses: dressmakers and mail order catalogues, department stores and high street multiple retailers who now sell cheaper, ready-to-wear fashion.

Manufacturing technology, too, has influenced fashion throughout the century. From the development of synthetic fabrics such as rayon and nylon to the advent of heat bonding and laser cutting, fashion designers have enthusiastically adopted new ways of creating beautiful clothes.

Despite fashion being big business, trends still filter up from street level. International designers send their scouts off to source ideas from clubs, markets and bars. But for the height of sartorial cool at any time of the year, one need look no further than the streets of London.

1 The *Belle Epoque*

1900–1914

Actress Carol McComas poses for the camera in 1905. Her clothes are typical of those of the elegant woman of the time, with an abundance of lace and frills and sweeping skirt. The waist was pulled in by corsets, and the bosom flung forward, but dress bodices fell loosely, billowing slightly over the waistband at the front. This would have been an evening dress, as high-collared dresses were always worn for day.

1 The *Belle Epoque*
1900–1914

The death of Queen Victoria in 1901 catapulted Britain into a new, light-hearted era. King Edward VII encouraged partying, consumerism and European travel. The British had a chance to catch up with the French, who had been enjoying the prosperous *Belle Epoque* since 1870. Paris was the fashionable centre of the Western world, boasting the couture houses of Callot Sœurs, Doucet, Drécoll, Worth and Paquin.

Despite this easier climate, women were slow to abandon their corsets. Their bodies were moulded into the 'S-bend' shape: bust out, hips back with the stomach smooth and flat. In her novel *The Edwardians* (1930) Vita Sackville-West describes Lucy, the Duchess, being fitted into heavily boned stays and suspenders: 'The lacing would follow, beginning at the waist and travelling gradually up and down, until the necessary proportions had been achieved.' Next came petticoats, stockings, drawers and pads to accentuate the hips. 'Button, gathering up the lovely mass of taffeta and tulle, held the bodice open while the Duchess flung off her wrap and dived gingerly into the billows of her dress.' It was a time-consuming business. The society woman's day was a whirl of dressing and re-dressing: from day dresses to visiting dresses to afternoon dresses. For paying calls in the morning she would wear tailor-made skirt suits, by designers such as John Redfern; taffeta-petticoated gowns which rustled provocatively were expected in the evening. Only the early evening tea-gown, for which couturier Lady Duff Gordon, 'Lucile', is remembered, allowed women to remove their corsets and retire to their boudoirs. ' "One of my off-days Rose. … Bring me the peach-blossom tea-gown, the new one, and the big embroidered cloak. I'm stifling in these woollen things," ' writes Colette in her novel *Chéri* (1920).

Designer Paul Poiret offered women some respite from corsets topped with lace and frills. After serving apprenticeships with an umbrella maker and with couture houses Doucet and Worth, he opened his own Paris house in 1903. Along with the house of Paquin, he introduced the Empire line and a more fluid silhouette. The waistline shot up to hang underneath the bust, and fabric fell in a softly draped column to the ground. The rigid whalebone stays vanished in favour of a more flexible tube corset which dropped to hold in the hips, freeing the bust. Poiret was delighted when, in 1909, Sergei Diaghilev's Ballets Russes came dancing into Paris. Léon Bakst's Eastern costumes for *Cléopâtre* and *Schéhérazade* had soon flooded the city in a wave of exoticism. Poiret, inspired by the oriental costumes and bright Fauvist colour, adopted a bold, theatrical style. He began offering soft tunics, harem pants, kimonos, turbans and long feathered plumes for the hair. Other Poiret innovations were cripplingly tight hobble skirts and lampshade dresses, with over-tunics flaring out from under the bust. In *The Age of Innocence*, published in 1920, Edith Wharton describes Newland Archer's pleasant surprise at his hostess' outfit: instead of 'a close-fitting armour of whale-boned silk . . . [she] was attired in a long robe of red velvet bordered about the chin and down the front with glossy black fur'. Always the forward-thinker, in 1911 Poiret was the first couturier to launch a fragrance, Rosine. He designed fabrics with painter Raoul Dufy and set up his own design school, the *École Martine*, which sold the fruits of its creativity in an adjoining shop.

Only the very rich could afford made-to-measure clothes from a couture house. Those without the budget commissioned dressmakers, shopped by mail order, bought patterns to sew at home or visited department stores. Selfridges took full-page advertisements in *The Times* and attracted more than 90,000 visitors to its opening in 1909, boasting 'prices we believe are the lowest in the world'. The competition for custom was fierce. Other stores like Debenham & Freebody advertised frantically in the days leading up to the opening, D.H. Evans claiming: 'Many imitate, but none excel.'

The fading popularity of the full corset coincided with a wider struggle for women's freedom. In London, suffragettes armed with umbrellas and hatpins fought with police and were thrown in gaol. In Rome, Pope Pius X condemned the wearing of low-cut evening dresses in front of men of the cloth, and in America women were arrested for wearing men's costumes when swimming.

With world conflict looming, fashion was soon to shed its frivolous streak as Europe geared up to dedicate its energy to the serious business of war.

Miss Sedley wears a delicately pleated, draped, high-necked gown, 1903. The twisting lines of the bodice emphasise the corseted curves of her silhouette, and her high collar would have been held up by wire or whalebone. Hairpieces and hair pads were often used to create the required volume, and hair was held in place with combs.

The décolleté style of these eveningwear dresses in this family portrait scandalously contrasts with the high necks worn during the day. The fussy 'frou-frou' detailing of frills, loose ribbons, lace and pleats were often set on a silk bodice base. This would give way to a wide cummerbund and a sweeping skirt with a train. Evening skirts were often decorated with flowers and tiers of pleated frills.

Women walk from Henley railway station to watch the Regatta during the 1905 Season armed with parasols and shawls. Summer day dresses were usually made in soft pastel colours such as lilac, white and pink, and these may have been made of printed cotton. Girls wore their hair long until they were eighteen, when it was swept up in combs and pins.

The Princess of Wales (centre), soon to become Queen Mary, attends a garden party at Marlborough House in 1907. The child on the far right, in the boater, is the future King George VI. Ostrich feathers were regarded as status symbols. Here they trim the ladies' hats and are worn draped around the shoulders. The sleeves of their intricately detailed dresses were typically cut slim and covered from the shoulder to the elbow with a wide, gathered over-sleeve.

The British actress Lillie Langtry was the mistress of the Prince of Wales, later to become King Edward VII. A noted beauty, the 'Jersey Lily' looks decidedly dowdy compared with her film star equivalents thirty years later; at the time, ostentatious make-up was considered vulgar.

Dancers from a musical play *The Dairymaids (1906)* demonstrate the fashionable S-bend shape, which was achieved by lacing women into metal or whalebone corsets. Pads placed on the hips and under the arms were used to emphasise a small, curved waist.

The corseted body shape that today looks deformed and unnatural was seen as the ideal womanly silhouette at the time. This hourglass figure belongs to actress Camille Clifford who was nicknamed the 'Gibson Girl'. Gibson Girls were originally characters created in the fashion illustrations of the American Charles Dana Gibson, but the term came to exemplify the independent sportswoman, with big hair and a tiny waist.

Camille Clifford came over from America and ended up marrying the son of Lord Aberdare. She was one of a small flock of glamorous, independent-minded American women who came over and injected money or beauty, and sometimes both, into British society.

This photograph of the actress Isabel Jay shows the opulent top of her dress, an example of the ornamental brocade and embroidery which was part of the craze for anything oriental. Silk flowers or rosettes were often placed on the high waistline on evening and day dresses.

A woman lifts her visiting dress just enough to show three rows of petticoats which were worn to keep the skirt in shape: cut tight over the hips it then flared out at the back. Before handbags became an essential accessory, women wore small purses or watches attached to a chain draped around the waist. Such chains were called chatelaines.

Bloomer-style bathing costumes hung out to dry in 1909 (above).
Sunbathing was not yet fashionable and a certain amount of
modesty was expected. Even paddling was a tricky business in
1902 with long, wide skirts and layers of petticoats, bloomers and
suspenders all determined to get in the way (opposite).

This fur-trimmed cape of 1902 was probably worn as eveningwear. Although the low-cut, frilled lace evening dress looks fragile, the frills would be set over a cage-like corset.

A beauty queen hides under a lavish cape from 1902. Long coats and skating outfits were some-times topped with a short, matching cape thrown over the shoulders. This one may have been part of a tea gown ensemble–long loose dresses and wraps which women relaxed in, without corsets, before dinner.

A gentlewoman would rarely be seen outside the house without her hat (and sometimes wore one inside), and together with long delicate parasols, a hat protected a lady from that vulgar notion, a suntan. Hats were usually pinned to the hair pads which sat below the natural hair to give it body. Fashionable hats were trimmed with flowers, fruit or feathers.

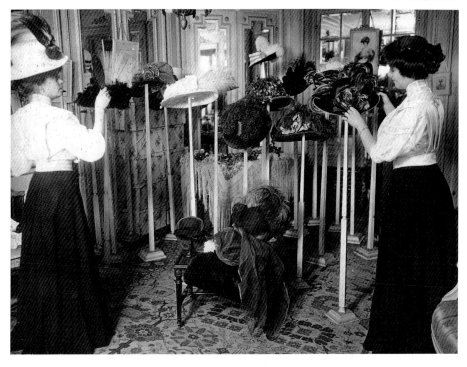

Two working women wear white shirts, or shirtwaisters, and long, dark skirts. This practical uniform was often worn for sports activities and was also taken up by teachers and women working in offices; in their way, they were an early equivalent of the Eighties power suit.

Miss Fundy poses in a long driving duster coat in 1912; probably
made of wool or gabardine, it is designed to protect her clothes.
Turbans were fashionable at the time and Paul Poiret had set the trend
as part of his craze for exotica. Driving was still considered to be a
dangerous sport and accidents were commonplace.

A 1906 competitor at Blackpool motor races. Women wore veils to protect their faces and to hold on their hats. This driver would also have needed a long duster coat for protection from the dirt. Goggles were sometimes worn and gloves were an essential part of a driver's wardrobe. Duster coats may have offered protection but they were particularly impractical.

A line-up of beauty queens from 1913 flaunt the modern Empire line with its high waistline (left). From left to right are the Misses England, France, Denmark, Germany, Italy and Spain. High necklines were replaced by stiffened lace collars which fastened at the back of the neck or as V-necks filled in with 'modesty panels'. The new streamlined style meant that society women could now dress themselves without the help of a maid. The sweeping skirts and wide hats of 1906 (above) must have seemed cumbersome in comparison.

Two women appear to hang onto every word of the future King George V (opposite) in 1907. The death of King Edward VII in 1910 flung the country into mourning. These women at Ascot (above) have translated their airy white dresses into mourning black with dyed hats, parasols and feathers to match. Women at the upper end of society would rarely have chosen to dress in black from head to toe if protocol had not demanded it.

Fashions influenced by Poiret included skirts worn daringly over harem pants (opposite) and opulently trimmed cloaks at Longchamp in 1914: this one is probably velvet. Dresses with ballooning panels which tapered at the thigh (above) were particularly popular in 1912 and 1913. The one on the left slims down to a tight, hobble-style skirt. Hobble skirts needed underwear which fettered the legs together, to make sure that the skirt was not stretched so that it ripped.

A French racegoer in 1912 wears a stream-lined dress with soft ballooning over-skirt, in a style similar to dresses designed by the house of Paquin. Madame Paquin (her real name was Jeanne Beckers) was one of the few female couturiers working at the time, and was known for her lavish dresses and pieces that combined drapery with tailoring.

Mrs Alice Keppel (centre), perhaps best known for being the mistress of King Edward VII, with her husband and daughter in 1907. The wind catches the feathers on her hat while her daughter holds firmly onto her own. Some hats were virtually turned into nests and sometimes used whole birds as decoration. The craze for the Orient is illustrated by the rich trim on Mrs Keppel's coat, which could have been a brocade.

The artist Vanessa Stephen was the novelist Virginia Woolf's sister; perhaps the only studio photograph for which she ever sat, this was probably taken on the occasion of her marriage to the art critic Clive Bell. Both were leading members of the Bloomsbury Group, a set of bohemian artists and writers. Vanessa Bell was known for wearing daringly bright, flowing robes but here she is more restrained in a simple dress.

Lady Ottoline Morrell, Bloomsbury Group society and literary hostess, sometimes wore extravagant Turkish robes and dyed her hair a soft purple. Here it is parted in the middle, swept up with combs, and probably pinned over hair pads to create the exaggerated rolls of hair which were fashionable at the time. Wherever she appeared, Lady Ottoline invariably caught the eye; Quentin Bell, the son of Clive and Vanessa Bell, described her as 'that fantastic, baroque flamingo…'

The neat, practical tailored suit evolved from menswear and was made fashionable by Queen Alexandra who ordered travel suits from master tailor John Redfern. Middle-class women wore them in the office and upper-class women wore them in the country. This S-bend 'tailor-made' of 1903 (right) evolved into a hobble skirt version (as worn by both women, (opposite) for 1914.

Sport in its many guises was now fashionable, and the rich had dedicated outfits for particular sports. Miss Hepburn's neat dress has a special ornate button at the waist, at which she has fastened her archery kit. She is drawing her bow at the Ladies' Day meeting of the Mid-Surrey Bowmen in Surbiton, that bastion of the genteel classes.

Mrs Albu makes a spirited return on the tennis courts of Knebworth House, Hertfordshire. Her large straw hat would have been securely pinned to the pads worn under her real hair. She wears tennis whites made up of a simple white shirt-waister and white skirt.

The 'great outdoors' had come into fashion, and women were going to have to exercise if they wanted to look svelte in their new Empire line gowns. Each sport still had its designated costume. Ms Kyle's golfing skirt (opposite) would have been made of tweed, and she may have added a matching Norfolk-style jacket. For skating (above) skirts were cut wide and fur was used to trim mufflers and long coats.

The actress Gladys Cooper, later to be the star of stage and screen in *The Second Mrs Tanquery* and *My Fair Lady*, wears a high-waisted Empire line evening dress in the new fluid, classical style. Although the fussy frills have gone, the surface of the dress is still intricately beaded. Feathers, tiaras and jewelled bands were often worn in the hair for the evening.

Actress Gertie Miller on stage in *The Dancing Mistress* of 1912 in full evening dress with long, white gloves, an essential eveningwear accessory. Dresses often had a small over-jacket incorporated into the garment like this one, which stops on the thigh, breaking the long column skirt into two tiers.

The Duncan dancers pose in classical costume, an influential fashion trend of the time. Isadora Duncan had caused controversy with her free-moving dance techniques that contrasted with the disciplined movement of classical ballet. She danced barefoot to the music of Brahms and Wagner and later founded her own dance school in Moscow.

The classical costume is translated into a fashionable Grecian-style dress of 1914. Designers Jacques Doucet, Paul Poiret and Mariano Fortuny all borrowed from the classical style, but this dress was probably a creation by designer Madeleine Vionnet who opened her house in Paris in 1912. She was famous for her bias-cut drapery and the influences of her style can be seen in the later work of Madame Grès and John Galliano.

The craze for the tango swept women off their feet, and in 1913 the German army was banned from doing the dance. Here Marguerite and Frank Gill demonstrate the Brazilian maxixe in 1914. Her dress is made for dancing, its slit skirts and draped armholes allowing easy movement. Popular tango shoes, like these in white satin, were trimmed with ribbon ankle straps. The house of Paquin was famous for its tango dresses.

Dancer Anna Pavlova demonstrates how freedom from the complete corset can mean freedom of movement. Her pleated dress may have been designed by Mariano Fortuny, who also dressed the dancer Isadora Duncan. Fortuny coloured dresses and cloaks with vegetable dyes and developed a sophisticated silk pleating technique. Ancient Greece helped to influence his famous pleated Delphos gown, which was tied to the body with a silk cord. In the 1980s the Japanese designer Issey Miyake continued the investigation into pleating techniques for his Pleats Please range.

Dancer Vera Fokina in the Ballets Russes production of *Schéhérazade* in 1910. The flamboyant Eastern-style costumes, which were designed by Léon Bakst, had a major influence on Paul Poiret and the houses of Worth and Paquin. Poiret introduced outfits in bright silks and brocades and sweeping feathers for the hair, and women at the time often wore ropes of pearls strung around the bodice.

The Fortuny-style pleating on this dress from 1909 has been incorporated into a more formal dress than Fortuny's loose tunic dresses. Fortuny dyed silks in graded colours, used Murano glass beads from Venice as decorative weights on hems and sleeves, and drew his inspiration from Ancient Greece and the Orient.

Actress Ina Claire
wears a dress that is
almost certainly the
famous 'lampshade'
dress designed by
Paul Poiret. The
floating circle of fur
that she touches
with her wrists
contrasts with the
smooth, draped
column line of the
dress which falls
from below the bust.
The hem would
have been wired to
make sure that it
stood away from the
body.

Two women wearing opera capes: (left) this one is designed
by Lady Duff Gordon and made from numerous individual
mole skins and, (right) black brocade inset with rose tafeta,
worn over a silver lamé dress. The lavish materials and
classical headdresses are typical of Poiret's style.

Actress Daisy Irving poses in what is probably a two-tiered 'lampshade' dress by Paul Poiret, 1910. His loose silhouettes reduced the need for as many underclothes as a 'frou-frou' dress would have done, and the bosom was freed from the confines of a corset.

Royal mistress Lillie Langtry demonstrates the fashion for slinging long beads or pearls over a low cut evening dress. Ornate jewels and tiaras decorated the hair for the evening. Miss Langtry is wearing a jewelled laurel wreath that makes reference to the trend for classicism. Her lavishly embellished and beaded dress may have come from one of the top couture houses, such as Jacques Doucet.

Queen Alexandra (above) wears a Cartier necklace in 1910. She was famous for wearing high chokers in the style shown and for wearing a daring amount of make-up, in so doing rejecting the fashion for natural complexions. The detailing on this elegant black dress (right) perfectly sets off the lavish jewellery worn around the neck.

The ballooning skirt of this day dress (above) tapers in to reveal two-tone leather boots which would have stopped just above the ankle. The parasol is trimmed with swan's down. Hobble skirts, introduced by designer Paul Poiret, were cut so tight that women had to take tiny steps to make any progress (right). They usually had tiered or single over-skirts and this one in black is by Biret.

The actress Gaby Deslys, famous for introducing Europe to American jazz, poses in the new Empire, or Directoire, line. The fluidity and ease of her dress, which is without frills, pleats or fussy trimmings, contrasts with the 'frou-frou' dresses of the early 1900s. Her skirt would have fallen in a streamlined column, and long ropes of pearls were particularly popular for evening dress.

2 Suited and Booted

1914–1919

A Parisienne takes a stroll with an army officer in 1916; she wears the new, relaxed wrap-style coat with its belt tied slightly above the natural waist and sensibly large pockets for times of war. Shorter skirts that showed off the ankles were more practical than the hobble skirts that restricted movement.

2 Suited and Booted
1914–1919

The outbreak of war in August 1914 cut short the wave of oriental extravagance. Fashion sobered up, with an emphasis on practicality, comfort and simplicity, as women learned to manage without their men or their maids. Relaxed, sporty dressing and dark coloured clothes (previously considered unladylike) came into fashion. Brassières, jumpers and masculine Norfolk-style skirt suits reflected the modern independent mood.

War dictated that women should now stride out rather than hobble. Fashion soon followed with the introduction of new wider flared skirts and hemlines which crept up to stop below the calf. The couturiers reacted to the restraints of the war, Jeanne Lanvin with relaxed chemise-dresses which were to become more popular in the 1920s, and the house of Paquin by combining drapery and tailoring for versatile day to evening dresses. Cloaks fell from the shoulders and jackets were belted just above the waist. Some fashion fads only touched those at the cutting edge: a revival of crinoline-style evening dresses and the frumpy barrel skirt that ballooned at the hips and tapered at the ankles. By 1918 waistlines had dropped to just above the hip.

One woman was to mark fashion history: Gabrielle Coco Chanel. A milliner based in Deauville, she dressed high society women fleeing the German advance on Paris and Northern France. Women who arrived without a stitch of clothing turned to Coco (a name Chanel acquired singing at a music hall) for straight skirts, sailor-style tops and simple hats. She went on to become a fashion pioneer, setting up a boutique in Biarritz and later establishing herself in Paris. The Chanel style shocked with its simplicity and offered women a casual elegance. Coco bought a run of jersey that had been rejected for the manufacturing of men's underwear and made short, straight skirts and streamlined, waistless dresses. Straight V-neck dresses were designed to tie at the hip with a scarf and belted jumpers, which, radically pulled over the head, were to be worn over simple skirts. Stylish, groomed and burning with ambition as she was, Chanel's own appearance was itself a successful promotional tool for her business. With Jean Patou she went on to introduce modern sports clothes as daywear, which redefined the way women dress.

In Britain, the war marked a turning-point for the equality of women. In 1918 married women over thirty were finally allowed the vote (women over twenty-one would have to wait until 1928) and in 1919 Nancy Astor was elected as the first female MP. No man could argue that they had not earned it. During the war the numbers of working women in Britain increased by 1.2 million; they were sent down mines, into factories and out to the fields, in addition to nursing, driving ambulances and doing office work. As a result of donning uniform, they threw away their romantic notions of fashion. They wore trousers and breeches, and tailored suits for the office.

During the post-war years women chose a more streamlined silhouette. In *Mrs Dalloway* (1925) Virginia Woolf writes: 'To his eye the fashions had never been so becoming; the long black cloaks; the slimness; the elegance; and then the delicious and apparently universal habit of paint. Every woman, even the most respectable, had roses blooming under glass; lips cut with a knife; curls of Indian ink.' Fashion was entering the Jazz Age.

Dame Ethel Mary Smyth, the British composer and suffragette, sporting a flat hat similar to the style worn for motoring which was fastened to the head with scarves. Her sporty tweed outfit, trimmed with velvet, might have been part of a tailored day suit or a sports jacket for an activity such as golf.

The suffragette Lady Emmeline Pethick-Lawrence wears a large duster coat, which she would have worn when out driving in an open-topped car. Duster coats were cut large and long so that they could wrap around the body to shield clothing.

Suffragettes in practical tailored suits and mannish ties do their bit for the cause. 1913 was the year the suffragettes held 'baby shows' to prove that they could both fight for the vote and be good mothers. The suffragette colours were purple, white and green, but many preferred simple suits and practical hats.

A suffragette recovers in police custody, 1940. She had fainted during a raid on Buckingham Palace where women, some armed with Indian clubs, had tried to break through a cordon of police in order to hand the King a petition. Her simple, bell-shaped skirt and tunic top, which may have tied with a sash at the back, shows how the ordinary woman would have dressed at the time.

Women workers in the Food Control Office sort sugar cards for distribution to the civilian population, 1917. Their uniform of long skirt and white shirt was sometimes accessorised with a man's-style knotted tie, as exemplified by the woman seated on the left in the photograph.

An Edwardian woman in 1917 also dresses in this practical style borrowed from the boys. Knotted bow ties were sometimes worn instead of the long ties that hung down the front of the shirt. Strands of pearls and the decorative pattern on the tie add a discreetly feminine touch.

The Women's Fire Brigade (above) in training for the job, wearing loose, protective dresses, 1916.
A young worker (opposite) mends army uniforms in America. Her sailor suit-style dress is typical of
childrenswear at the time. Boys would have worn a similar top, but with trousers. The bows which
girls wore in their hair became known as 'flappers' because of the way they fell onto the head. The
name would stick with this generation, as they grew up in the Twenties.

A line of policewomen, newly recruited for duty, at a munitions works,
1917. Some women wore trousers for this sort of work. It was against
the rules to wear anything that contained metal when undertaking
munitions work; this included metal supports in corsets. By 1915 many
women were working twelve-hour days in factories for the war effort.

The same policewomen recruits pose in their civilian clothes, at first glance little different from uniforms. The stern line is broken up only by two women wearing opulent fur coats.

The trench coat, an essential part of a soldier's uniform, was soon adopted by civilian men and women. They were made of beige cotton mixes or wool, and detailing included a sturdy belt and storm cuffs. These lightweight coats could easily be thrown over a tailored suit or dress, and might be bought from companies such as Burberry. Later on, trench coats or mackintoshes became standard commuter fare, and were worn over a suit for travelling to work.

A London woman greets an American soldier as he marches
through the capital in 1917. The skirt of her softly tailored
summer suit may have been made from linen and a minute
row of buttons may also have run down the front of her
jacket to match those on her sleeve.

An American soldier says goodbye to his girl at home in 1917. Upright feathers on hats were fashionable at the time and were also used to decorate turbans and bicorne hats. This woman's loose jumper-blouse was a new, relaxed piece introduced by Chanel which pulled over the head and fastened with a loose sash at the waist. The white cuffs and collar are very typical of Chanel. She wears practical lace-up boots.

Austrian women bid farewell to mobilised troops in 1914. Short-brimmed and brimless hats were typically softened with fabric scarves and felt petals. The tasselled bag held by the woman on the left would have been constructed using a metal frame. By then the silhouette had loosened up and simplified, with loose skirts and easy coats, or tailored skirt suits. The waistline had almost fallen back to its natural place once again.

Department stores were where the middle-class woman could go to buy her clothes 'off the peg', including the latest Paris copies. Some stores also had dressmaking departments. These female lift operators at Swan and Edgar in London's Piccadilly wear braid-trimmed uniforms.

Doorkeepers at Selfridges in Oxford Street, one of London's most famous department stores, 1915. They are dressed in long, practical duster-style coats, probably in beige, with small logos at the cuff. When Selfridges opened in 1909, the public was warned not to tip the doormen or staff.

Christmas shoppers outside Bourne & Hollingsworth in London's Oxford Street in 1919. As well as going to department stores, women could order clothes and accessories from mail order catalogues.

A queue forms for a film at the New Gallery cinema in 1918. Charlie Chaplin films and newsreels made popular viewing at the time. The simple lines of women's suits and coats make the clothes of the older woman (right of the picture) in her fussy *Belle Epoque*-style cape look dated. Hats were no longer so flamboyant and simple styles became everyday wear.

This 'clippie', wearing a short skirt and braided trim jacket, cheerfully takes on the role of bus conductor, a job usually given to a man, 1917. Her flared skirt is of a similar shape to women's daywear skirts of the time, but it is cut much shorter. As if in deference to modesty, her boots go further up her leg than those worn for civilian dress.

Two of the many women who replaced male porters at London's Marylebone Station in 1915 (opposite). Their pinafore-style overalls were worn for practical purposes to protect their long, dark dresses. Pinafore-wrap dresses became a fashionable style for women during the 1940s. This female guard (right) on the Metropolitan Railway wears a skirt that is daringly short for 1916. Her long boots and tight, nipped-in jacket look very modern compared with the long, loose suits which women wore when out of uniform. This streamlined style would not be taken up for everyday wear until the 1920s.

Women of the WAAC take to the dance floor in 1918. Large pockets with leather buttons and high-belted waistlines were also a popular detail on civilian clothing.

Sacrificing their feminine tresses (and clothes) for the cause, these Russian women are possibly part of the thousand-strong Women's Death Battalion which tried to protect the provisional government meeting in the Winter Palace in Petrograd when the Bolsheviks stormed the building in 1917.

Women forestry workers sharpen their axes in 1918, wearing masculine-style breeches (opposite); a Land Girl, also in breeches, vaults athletically over a gate (right). Women were allowed to adopt more practical masculine clothing for war work. They now wore brassières and in 1916 the first birth control clinic was opened in America. With so many men away at the war, who was there to complain?

Armaments factory workers in about 1916 (opposite). They are wearing trousers, something previously unheard of for women. Caps keep their hair out of the way of the dangerous work they are likely to be undertaking. Post Office workers (above) display the uniform of the working woman during the war, a shirtwaister and long skirt. The woman on the far right shows off her tiny waist with a neat sash and demonstrates the new silhouette, with its high waist and flared, loose skirt.

The first woman bus driver marries a soldier in 1916 (above); both are in the uniform of their trade. Women also wore cream silk suits teamed with wide hats as an alternative to the traditional wedding dress (opposite). Dresses were high-waisted, and often had a V-neck tunic-style bodice which fell over a skirt; wax and silk flowers were used to trim net veils. As couples were reunited at the end of the war, weddings boomed.

Women expose their fur trims and mufflers to the wet weather, braving the elements to pose with war hero Captain Ball VC. The woman on the left carries a small bag, which could have been made of metal mesh and lined with brightly coloured satin, a fashionable style at the time. Her bell-shaped coat contrasts with the more flared version of the woman on the right. Both shapes were popular during the war.

Crowds in America celebrate the end of the war in 1918. Now that skirts were shorter, women often wore boots rather than shoes, with lace-up or button-up fastenings. Canvas panels were sometimes used for boot uppers to economise on leather, giving a two-tone effect, as worn by both women giving their soldier boy a lift.

Partying at the Ritz Hotel, London, on the first anniversary of the
Armistice, November 1919. For evening, women wore loosely draped V-
neck column dresses under kimono-style wrap coats, which were
sometimes detailed with tasselled ties. Fans, feathered headdresses and
long, white gloves were the right accessories for more lavish evening
events.

The jumper-blouse in cotton or silk was a style which Chanel helped to make fashionable, and offered women a comfortable alternative to a shirt, bodice or tunic top. They were slipped over the head rather than fastened with buttons or tied on, and tied at the waist with a sash. In this photograph Mrs Whiple is shown in just such an outfit at home in her conservatory.

A woman relaxes in a softly tailored jacket and wide skirt, 1916. The clothing creates a silhouette that is almost identical to the skirt and jumper shown opposite.

These bathing costumes of 1918 are probably made out of knitted wool. For the sake of modesty, drawers were sometimes covered with skirts, and caps or headscarves were used to protect the hair. The cap on the left looks as if it is made out of rubber.

The Prince of Wales and his party are snapped by eager Royal-watchers in 1919. War and the designs of Coco Chanel had helped to break down the class barriers as exemplified by dress codes. Society women now worked and, when their servants left to join the war effort, as many did, they adopted a more simple fashion style. White cotton dresses were worn by both upper- and working-class women. Those seen here were possibly made of satin, and tucks and folds running across the skirts were a popular detailing trend.

(Above) Sporting ladies wear their tennis whites at The Queens Club in London in 1918. The sleek jumper-blouse (above, left) worn by the woman on the right was probably made of knitted silk. Tennis outfits were similar to golfing outfits (opposite), but a plain skirt replaced the pleats and lace-up shoes were worn instead of slip-ons. Shoulder bags were not widely used for daywear, but the one carried by the woman in the middle may have held golf balls.

The Harrodian ladies' football team lines up at Barnes, in London, on a cold November day. If breeches were allowed for the war effort, then why not shorts for sport? The wool caps, similar in shape to those worn for factory work and swimming, kept the girls' hair tucked away and off their faces.

Guests arrive at Buckingham Palace (above), the woman on the right wearing an opulent scarf around her dress, 1919. White would come to be accepted as a colour suitable for mourning, since by the end of the war so many men were dead, but efforts were also made to produce more fashionable clothing in black. Cloaks were thrown around the shoulders for evening and more formal occasions (opposite); the one shown is a particularly lavish number in velvet and fur.

Hats were now being worn in styles that fitted the head more closely, as in this feathered creation from 1919. A woman without a hat was still not considered to be fully dressed, and fashionable styles included structured turbans adorned with feathers and toques that rose up in triangular point above the forehead. The woman in this picture is dressed in relaxed daywear; her wrap top is similar to the jersey styles promoted by Chanel.

For lazy days away from the horrors of the war, wide
straw hats, cotton summer dresses and music by the
riverside were just the thing.

This lavish coat, made in Paris, is cut in the popular curved, bell-shaped silhouette of about 1916 (*left*). Military braiding and frogging became fashionable as a trim on womenswear (*opposite*). This woman also wears a fashionable bicorne hat. She might have been wearing a tubular-shaped skirt underneath, which became the most fashionable shape of 1919.

Hair was sometimes parted in the middle and swept into a chignon at the back, but the most modern styles were bobbed and waved like this one (left), a style that sat neatly under the popular, close-fitting hats. (Opposite) Socialite Lady Diana Cooper wears her hair short in 1916. Her long beads, headband and loosely draped dress are reminiscent of the easy classical styles promoted by Paul Poiret and Madeleine Vionnet.

3 Boom and Bust

1920–1929

Talking to the water. Poling away from the jetty,
this girl has gone punting wearing a sporty dress
cut in the straight up and down garçonne style
popular in the mid-Twenties. Scarves and cloche
hats were fashionable accessories.

3 Boom and Bust

1920–1929

In all walks of life, the 1920s celebrated youth and life after the dark war years. Fashion was no exception. As if to compensate for the deaths of so many young men, an androgynous 'bachelor girl' silhouette emerged. Skirts became daringly short, breasts were flattened with bandeaus and waistlines were slung on the hip. Women smoothed their hair into a short shingle or a boyish Eton crop, then hid it under a tight cloche hat.

Chanel's designs epitomised this 'borrowed from the boys' look, with nautical sailor trousers, reefer jackets and blazers as well as more classic pyjamas, open-necked shirts and jumpers. Her cardigan suit and more feminine 'little black dress' have remained timeless classics. Why should a girl wear diamonds when she could wear string upon string of fake pearls? Chanel made costume jewellery acceptable and created Chanel No. 5, a fragrance which (unfashionably for the time) smelt nothing like a flower.

Fashion continued to hang loose. Women needed to exercise to stay slim and wanted clothes in which they could move and dance. The great outdoors were in fashion and Jean Patou opened a sports shop and made clothing for the golf course, the piste and the tennis court. He designed sporty, elegant resortwear that was minimal but easily recognisable when emblazoned with his JP logo of 1924. In addition, Patou livened up his clothing by borrowing geometric motifs from the thriving 1920s art scene, namely Cubism and Art Deco.

The fashion industry was not forgotten at the 1925 Exhibition of Decorative Art in Paris. The womenswear market was specifically targeted in a move that was unusual for the time. The visitor could see jewellery by Boucheron and Cartier and admire the work of couture houses Jenny, Paquin and Vionnet. Couturier Jeanne Lanvin showed off her interior design skills and, on the Seine, Poiret filled three barges with modern furniture and textiles.

The Roaring Twenties brought with them a passion for the jazz music of Jelly Roll Morton, night-clubbing at Le Bœuf sur le Toit in Paris and dancing the Bunny Hug and the Kickaboo.. ' "Oh, Nina, what a lot of parties."… (Masked parties, Savage parties, Victorian parties, Greek parties, Wild West parties, Russian parties, Circus parties… dull dances in London and comic dances in Scotland and disgusting dances in Paris).' wrote Evelyn Waugh in *Vile Bodies* (1930), his novel about the 'Bright Young Things' of the 1920s. As the skirts went up, morals went down, and doctors warned that women were turning to cigarettes and alcohol to fuel their debauched lifestyles. Where the term 'flapper' had once described debutantes before they 'came out', now it referred to any young woman obsessed with dancing the Charleston to the frenetic sounds of Bix Beiderbecke, dressed in rolled-down stockings, T-bar shoes and short skirts.

Not every woman wanted to look like a flapper, however. The harsh Twenties cut only flattered those with a boyish, adolescent figure. Because chemise dresses and jersey separates were stark and unforgiving, women would soften the look with beading and opulent fabrics. They piled on the bracelets, scarves, hats and feathers. Selfridges stocked coloured beads 100 centimetres long, and, in an advertisement in *The Times*, explained: 'Usually only three shades are worn: to match, to tone and to contrast with one's gown.' At the end of the decade shapes became softer and clung to the figure, rather than ignoring the natural curves. Designer Madeleine Vionnet made bias-cut, fluid dresses for the more womanly silhouette by draping, gathering and twisting fabric so that it swept over the body in a classical style. She realised her ideas on miniature dolls before working full-scale and was a forerunner of the bias-cut glamour dresses that became fashionable in the Thirties.

The words of Jean Cocteau in his 1921 novel *The Miscreant* were remarkably prescient: 'Fashions die young. That is what makes their gaiety so grave.' In 1927 dancer Isadora Duncan strangled to death as her scarf tangled in the wheels of her sports car. This sinister fashion moment pre-empted the end of an era. On Black Thursday, 24 October 1929, the Wall Street Crash brought the world economy tumbling down, marking the beginning of the Great Depression. Life looked set to be tough, and, ever in tune with the times, Patou made the hemline fall, too.

This opulent embroidered dress of 1922 (left), designed by Melnotte Simonine, has a matching cape-like wrap. Capes which were cut long and fell vertically from the shoulders with just two slits for arms were fashionable and were sometimes executed in thicker, less decorative fabric for warmth. Women often wore flimsy printed dresses (opposite) and close-fitting hats for formal summer occasions such as the Royal Garden Party at Buckingham Palace. The dress worn by the woman on the left could have been made of silk or the synthetic, rayon.

Long, wide-skirted 'picture dresses', or *robes de style*, offered a feminine look at the beginning of the Twenties, and were often executed in pastel colours. The dress with a floating, panelled skirt (opposite) and the dress with the bow sash (above, right) are both by couturier Jeanne Lanvin, who was particularly known for her beaded and embroidered picture dresses. The fern-printed dress (worn by the woman on the left) is by the house of Jenny and is worn with a chain ankle bracelet. *Robes de style* were often worn with wide straw hats and this one (above left, woman on the right) is trimmed with a silk flower.

The bold printed textiles of these 1921 dresses help to break up the silhouette, and matching parasols emphasise the prints. The early Twenties brought with it a softer style: skirts often fell wide from a dropped waist, and sweeping cloaks were worn over dresses for evening. Fashion had not yet given way to the straight up and down look.

Folk art motifs were used on dresses and coats as detailing, and they appear on the skirt of this *robe de style* (above, left). So as not to make this crinoline-style dress (above, right) seem heavy, designer Jean Patou has used thin, semi-transparent fabric, showing a double-layered underskirt underneath and light embroidered detailing. Rosettes and circular ribbon motifs were popular at the time (above, centre), and small purse bags were often attached to pieces of clothing disguised as bunches of flowers.

Robes de style looked romantic, while chemise dresses were sleeker and less overtly feminine. This dress (above, left) uses sheer fabric, frilled cuffs and floral embellishment to create a sense of fussy femininity, whereas the frills and flowers on this square-cut dress (above, right) are used to soften what could have been a very minimal shape. The bands of print continue the tiered effect up to the neckline.

Racegoers on the first day of Ascot in 1926. The bold geometric outfit of the woman on the right contrasts with the delicate pleated dress of her friend. The former wears a suit which, although it follows the wide-skirted lines of a typical *robe de style*, is without the feminine frills and delicate organza associated with the look.

At the Ascot races a woman prepares to put up
her umbrella against the rain in 1926. When the
weather was sunny, however, parasols were no
longer essential accessories, as having a suntan
was now becoming fashionable.

At Ascot in 1928 the woman on the right has chosen to wear a softer, more elegant dress with sheer and floral detailing similar to the picture dresses fashionable at the beginning of the Twenties. Her wide straw hat is more suited to this look than a sleek cloche might be.

An androgynous model wears a velvet coat designed by Jane. The frogging fastenings and braided pockets were fashions that had continued from the First World War, where they were references to military dress. Chanel was known for her more simple cardigan-style braid-edged jackets. The model's hat is made of felt, and her lips are exaggeratedly made up into the fashionable 'bee-sting' shape.

Two coats decorated with ornamental buttons are worn with cloche hats. Jeanne Lanvin produced dresses with rows of round steel buttons, and these may well be by her. Lanvin was made famous by selling matching mother-and-daughter outfits before the war, and during the Twenties she moved on to Aztec embroidery and dinner pyjamas.

The little black dress was made fashionable by Coco Chanel and Edward Molyneux and was promoted by American *Vogue* in 1926. Black dresses had not previously been fashionable for society women, unless they were in mourning. For one thing, they made a good base from which to show accessories. A velvet dress by the house of Jenny (above, left), another dress by Jenny showing off a tasselled lipstick holder (above, centre), and a dress by Madeleine Vionnet (above, right) with signature scalloped panels.

The plain black dress by Bernard (above, left) draws attention to the rosette motif at the hip and the decorative buckles on the shoes. An embroidered belt has matching cuff detail (above, centre) which resembles a fashionable row of bracelets. The dress is by the House of Jenny. The tiered pleats of *crêpe de chine* of this Phillippe & Gaston dress (above, right) help to soften the silhouette.

The long, white evening gown by Norman Hartnell (left), 1924, might well have been aimed at the debutante market. Classical drapery would be taken up again as a trend in the 1930s by Madeleine Vionnet. Dancer Irene Castle (opposite) poses in a classical-style dress, 1922.

The class of 1927. Debutantes take lessons in how to curtsey
elegantly when presented at Court. The trick was to keep your
balance without showing your underwear or tripping on your dress.
The ostrich feather fans may have been a reference to the Prince of
Wales's feathered insignia.

Joan Gatti arrives at Buckingham
Palace in 1929 to be presented to the
Queen. The occasion demanded a
formal white dress with a train and
she is dressed accordingly.

French tennis star Suzanne Lenglen reaches to make a return at Wimbledon in 1922. Her daringly rolled-down stockings in the 'flapper' style had the more conservative members of society tut-tutting, and her on- and off-court wardrobe was designed by master sports designer Jean Patou.

Couturier Jean Patou (left) was renowned for his sporty clothes. The clean lines of the summer dress worn by his companion are subtly broken up by a feminine scarf. This is a very good example of how the leisure look of the war had evolved into a simpler style by the 1920s.

The Dolly sisters, with Madame de Brissac centre, dressed in relaxed resort-style clothing at Deauville in 1922. The suit on the right could have been trimmed with braid, and may have been by Chanel, who had a boutique in Deauville. The white dress is reminiscent of tennis dresses worn at the time, but this Dolly sister is unlikely to have played tennis in her high heels.

(Right) The 1924 Diaghilev Ballets Russes *Le Train Bleu*, costumed by Chanel, shows the quintessential sportswear fashions of the 1920s. The role of the tennis player, danced by Bronislava Nijinska, was inspired by French tennis star Suzanne Lenglen, who is pictured (above) the same year at Wimbledon with René Lacoste (of crocodile logo fame). The costume of the golfer, danced by Leon Wozikowsky, on the left, was inspired by outfits worn by the dapper Prince of Wales. The other dancers, Lydia Sokolova and Anton Dolin, are dressed in jersey bathing costumes.

Tennis player Dorothea Lambert Chambers teaches the backhand to two of her pupils in
1921. The high waistlines and bell skirts of these simple dresses are similar to wartime styles.
The white dresses help to set off their fashionable suntans.

Film star Gloria Swanson wears a Suzanne Lenglen-style headband, and shows off her perfect curls and eyebrows plucked almost to nothing.

When Tutankhamen's tomb was discovered in 1922, fashion reacted by creating a craze for things Ancient Egyptian. This tunic-style dress (left) is decorated with Egyptian hieroglyph motifs. There was also a fashion for anything in the Chinese style, as illustrated by this opulent silk dress by Rolande (opposite, left), and accessories in the style included Chinese brocade bags. The skirt panel of bold florals of this 1925 coat (opposite, right) pulls the eye down the body to the hip and away from the waist, so emphasising the drop-waisted, boyish cut.

The schoolgirl look outfit worn by the woman on the right is an example of the boyishly cut 'flapper' separates favoured during the Twenties, and her andro-gynous accessories include a beret and a tie. Her cardigan is probably made of jersey. The checked dress worn by her companion on the left is by Parry, 1925.

Two women model the latest fashions in Deauville, August 1925. Chanel favoured nautical-style references in her clothing, as well as blazers and straight skirts, and these two outfits could well have been designed or influenced by her. The woman on the right displays a very short Eton crop haircut; women sometimes used brilliantine to achieve a slick shine for their short hair.

A well-groomed Coco Chanel poses in her signature style: an easy cardigan suit, two-tone shoes, strings of pearls, and bobbed hair, a look which is still a classic of today.

This picture (and the one opposite) was taken in 1929, when Chanel was forty-six, the year in which she opened an accessories boutique attached to her Paris salon. The pearls on the pin trimming her straw hat are extra large. Chanel played with oversized costume jewellery that did not pretend to be real.

Straight up and down jersey separates (opposite) are typical Chanel style. This outfit is by the Mattita fashion house. The V-neck jumper of this streamlined, hand-knitted suit is in rust-coloured silk (above, left). Tasselled bags complemented the fringed dresses of the era and cloche hats, softened with veils or turban styles, were worn at the end of the decade. This knitted wrap (above, right) reflects the drop-waisted cuts of the era with its hip-height stripe.

The Paquin knitted loose dress and matching knitted coat are examples of the loose, unstructured dressing which women enjoyed. The graphic patterns make references to the modern art movements happening at the time.

These outfits by Wilson's of Great Portland Street, London, make a direct reference to the pioneering styles of Chanel and Patou. Chanel introduced jersey dressing, such as the cardigan suit on the right, and similar outfits were worn when playing golf. But it was Patou who used graphic sporty lines and even logos on his designs.

The print of this graphically bold dress of 1927 has borrowed ideas from the Art Deco geometric patterns seen on the lacquered vases of Jean Dunand and the textiles of the painter and designer Sonia Delaunay.

Ballet dancer Kyra Alanova wears an exotic dress perhaps made from textiles designed or influenced by Sonia Delaunay or from Poiret's *Ecole Martine*.

(Left) This outfit of 1929 is similar to one of Jeanne Lanvin's Breton suits whose short, braided jacket was decorated with buttons and worn over a white collared shirt with a red bow. (Opposite) Walking frocks of 1925 use thick, sporty stripes and rich oriental patterns in addition to the fashionable button decoration. The cloche hat on the left is loosened into a turban style.

Edith Wilson dances the Black Bottom from the London show *Blackbirds* in 1928 (opposite). Her square-cut dress allows for maximum movement and is decorated with a linear motif influenced by the Art Deco movement. (Right) World champion Charleston dancer Bee Jackson wears a beaded and fringed dance dress, popular at the time, as the fringes would shimmer and shake and draw attention to movement. This dress is shorter than the typical styles of the era. Paste jewellery known as 'slave bracelets' was often worn high up on the arm as well as at the wrist.

Champion Charleston dancer Gwendlyn
Graham with the chorus of the revue
Blackbirds. They rehearse in jersey leotards,
similar to bathing costumes worn at the time,
and a style that Claire McCardell was to revisit
in the 1940s. Their rolled-down stockings were
associated with dancing and 'flapper' style and
were considered *risqué*.

Joan Crawford poses against an Art Deco-style backdrop in 1929 (right). The bold make-up and close-cropped curls tucked under a cloche hat (opposite) were considered modern, and by now smoking was deemed acceptable for women.

Exotic harem pant pyjamas (above), first introduced to Paris by Poiret (shown here in 1922), were worn as eveningwear throughout the Twenties. English writer Marguerite Radclyffe Hall (opposite, standing) whose novel *The Well of Loneliness* (1928) was banned for its pro-lesbian stance, poses with Lady Una Trowbridge in 1927. The man's-style evening jacket is a precursor of Yves Saint Laurent's famous *Le Smoking*.

Hollywood actress Gilda Grey (Marianna Michalska) wears a beaded evening dress with white fox fur trim, by Lucien Lelong. Dance dresses were often opulently beaded, embroidered and fringed. Long ropes of pearls and diamanté jewellery were popular accessories, and opulent buckles, like the ones seen on Grey's shoes, helped to draw attention to the legs – the new erogenous zone. Gilda Grey is credited with inventing the dance called the Shimmy.

Actress Binnie Hale wears a gold lamé evening dress in the London show *No No Nanette*, 1925. Lamé was made by weaving metallic thread into fabric, and was popular in both gold and silver along with rich brocades.

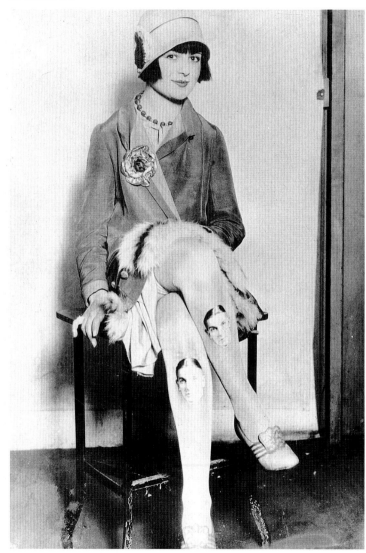

A Baltimore girl wears her boyfriend's photograph on her stockings. As hemlines rose, attention was focused on stockings and shoe fashions. Ribbed and patterned stockings were fashionable, such as checked tights for sports, and stockings were made out of cotton, wool, silk or rayon. Patterned legs would be popular again, but not until they accompanied mini-skirts in the Sixties.

Stockings held up by decorative metal garters, to match gold kid evening shoes. Band garters became popular in addition to suspender garters, and young women and dancing 'flappers' scandalised their elders by rolling down their stocking tops so that they could be seen just above the knee.

Out in the country, two women march through a Devon field with their spoils, looking like naughty schoolboys (above). Jumpers that pull over the head were worn for sportswear until Chanel promoted them for daywear, and shorts were only worn for sporting events. These girls (opposite) are borrowing from the boys; their tweed Norfolk jackets and plus-fours were traditionally worn by men for sporting events. Scarves were often worn tied around the head instead of hats, for a leisure look.

Golfing clothes for women in 1921 (above) combine simple linen or jersey skirts, straw hats and V-neck knitted jumpers. These easy clothes, flexible enough to allow a decent swing, were made fashionable by Chanel and Patou. Winston Churchill (opposite) and his son Randolph share a joke with Coco Chanel at a meet of the Mimizan Hunt in 1928; the hounds belonging to the Duke of Westminster, with whom Chanel was having an affair at the time. She was renowned for appearing groomed and elegant at all times.

The Debenham sisters pull up on their motorcycles for a quick
gasper, 1925. The one on the right wears lace-up shoes,
woollen stockings and jodhpurs or breeches, an outfit also
associated with horse and bicycle riding. The striped knits are
modern jumpers, adapted from a man's wardrobe.

A contestant in a 1923 motorcycle race checks her lipstick. By now it was acceptable for women openly and obviously to wear make-up and to paint their faces in public. Eyebrows were plucked and made up to look arched and high, lips were painted red and shaped into a 'Cupid's bow', and cheeks were rouged.

The American Amelia Earhart was famous for her flights across the Atlantic and Pacific oceans. She disappeared without trace in an attempt to fly around the world. This picture, taken in 1928, shows Earhart dressed in warm leather military-style boots and coat with a close-fitting hat, similar to the cloche shapes fashionable at the time.

Two women drivers at Brooklands racetrack in Surrey, 1920. Women no longer wore sweeping duster coats and veils for riding in cars, but instead sported streamlined coats of a more practical length, loosely based on the trench coat.

(Opposite) Knitted St Moritz ski fashions, 1924; man's-style plus-fours and breeches were popularised by women for skiing during the Twenties. Jean Patou was particularly known for his skiwear but this two-piece jersey suit of 1926, modelled in Chamonix (right), is made by Chanel. Ski pant-style leg warmers hook under the skates for additional comfort and warmth for the wearer.

The elegant flapping panel jacket and matching dress in grey georgette (opposite) are by Lucien Lelong. Lelong was known for his luxurious fabrics and fine craftsmanship, and went on to be president of the *Chambre Syndicale de la Haute Couture* in 1937, the body which represents Paris couturiers. The grey lace and silk dress (right) is reminiscent of a child's pinafore dress from the beginning of the century.

This floral print dress with velvet and chiffon scarf panels would have been worn in the second half of the Twenties when hems were cut to look uneven, in a move away from the boyish silhouette. Although cloche hats were more fashionable, wide hats were often worn for more formal events.

This 1925 floral printed dress by Blanche Lebouvier, trimmed with velvet and chiffon, was cut in a similar style to evening dresses of the time, with a bow detailing which often rested on the side of the hip or at the front, as shown in this photograph.

Ever-elegant Gertrude Lawrence wears a dress with a soft draped neck line and pointed scarf hem, typical of the late Twenties (right). The romantic, almost child-like, dress (opposite) was worn by actress June (Lady Inverclyde) in the musical comedy *Happy-Go-Lucky*. The nautical white collars and cuffs and ribbon detail borrow from sports and leisurewear styles, and scalloped hems were particularly fashionable at the end of the decade.

Max Factor instructs English film star Dorothy MacKaill in the art of applying her make-up (opposite). Actress Evelyn Brent is helped by her assistant (above). Max Factor was employed by Hollywood to make up the stars, and can claim responsibility for dyeing Jean Harlow's hair blonde in the 1930s. For black and white films he used black make-up on lips and eyes to create a contrast to the heavy white base. He later set up his own line of cosmetics, whose name survives to this day.

Models keep warm in their brightly coloured beach wraps and rubberised bathing hats in 1928 (above). This picture was not shot on a beach, but on the roof of an Oxford Street store in London. Plenty of sunshine and fresh air was considered healthy. These simple beach dresses of 1927 (opposite) are livened up by bright prints and matching hats.

A woman poses in a brightly embroidered swimming costume by Sonia Delaunay. Delaunay, who was married to artist Robert Delaunay, produced bright graphic designs, inspired by Cubist paintings, for the textile company Bianchini-Ferier. In 1925, Delaunay set up a boutique selling rugs, screens and handbags. She shared the shop with furrier Jacques Heim, who was to set up his own couture house in 1930.

Swimming costumes were made of knitted cotton or wool. In 1920 the American company Jantzen designed elasticised costumes in rib knits; this meant that they held their shape better when wet. This piece may well have been by Jean Patou or Elsa Schiaparelli, both of whom designed costumes with graphic patterns.

These American girls cool down and play cards sitting on blocks of ice on a hot day in August 1929 (left). The low, sweeping backs and cutaway panels offer maximum suntan advantages. This style was developed towards the end of the decade. (Above) A beach inspector at West Palm Beach measures the bathing suit to ensure it conforms to regulations.

The Mack Sennett Bathing Belles show off the latest fashionable bathing costumes, although the fur-trimmed version would probably not benefit from exposure to sea water.

Marcel Grateau, who pioneered the hair wave technique, shows how it is done in 1922. These painstakingly created waves offered a softer alternative for women used to the more masculine Twenties crop. The style was to take off during the Thirties, as it complemented the full-length, feminine dresses and elegant day suits. The Twenties brought with it bold make-up, including nail varnish, mascara and dark, kohl-lined eyes.

Polish-born hair-dresser Antoine, seen on the right, is credited with creating the fashionably short shingle cut. Based in Paris, he experimented with coloured wigs and hair dyes and created his own haircare and cosmetics ranges. His clients included Josephine Baker and Greta Garbo.

In the 1920s hair was cropped shorter and shorter in the shingle cut, short, sharp bobs and the Eton crop, the severest of all. Only towards the end of the decade did softer, longer waves become more fashionable. Louise Brooks's bob (right) was particularly influential.

(Opposite, from left to right, top to bottom) a variety of styles: Gloria Swanson – a softer waved bob; Joan Crawford – a longer curled style; Jessie Matthews – a Louise Brooks-style bob; Clara Bow – the original 'It' girl, a longer, more feminine curled style; Yvonne Printemps – a softer waved bob; Pauline Stark – a boyish short cut; Constance Talmadge – Eton crop meets bob; Josephine Baker – a boyish short cut; Madame Lucien Lelong – a softer waved bob.

Pyjamas were worn for evening and on the beach, and particularly well known were the printed silk versions by designer Edward Molyneux. During the Twenties they were also worn as nightwear and as loungewear, a modern version of the tea-gown of the *Belle Epoque*. Opulent brocade shawls like the one on actress Thalia Barbarova's chair (opposite) were popular, with some of the most luxurious coming from France.

This more traditional nightdress echoes the V-neck shape of fashionable dresses of the time, and is provocatively tied at the shoulder with ribbons.

The introduction of rayon, a synthetic alternative to silk, meant that more women could afford this elegant loungewear pyjama look. These pyjamas are made of crepe satin and trimmed in lace.

Models display a range of corsets at Oxford Street's Dorothy Perkins store in 1925. Whalebone corsets were long gone for most women, but elasticised stretch corsets were worn either over the hips with a silk camisole top or sometimes over the full torso. Bras were also worn with cami-knickers as a more comfortable alternative.

This slip (above, left), which was probably made of silk, is combined with matching long knickers. One-piece camisoles became popular for the first time in the Twenties; this one (above, right) was probably in cotton, trimmed with lace and worn under a waist-slimming corset.

This bloomer-style outfit (above, left) from 1928 would have been a two-piece rather than an all-in-one. This very luxurious underwear (above, right) is made up of an accordion-pleated lace under-slip, trimmed with chiffon and ermine-tailed rosettes.

Cloche hats would sit smoothly on the head and mimicked the fashionable boyish hairstyles of the era. Turn-up brims helped to soften the face, as in the one worn by Greta Garbo (top, left), and more minimal felt styles were trimmed with felt or silk flowers (top, right) and as worn by Anita Loos (above, right). Straw cloches were decorated with bands at the end of the decade (above, left).

Wide, romantic straw shepherdess-style hats were worn to the races and at the beach, and trimmed with ribbons or silk flowers, as worn by actress Virginia Valli (top, left and above, right). Softer turban-style cloches (above, left) and scarf detailing (top, right) offered an alternative to minimal helmet styles.

Lady Edwina Mountbatten with her daughter Patricia wears a boyishly streamlined skirt and matching top for a 1928 wedding. This is an excellent example of the simpler lines of the late 1920s, and the outfit is probably made of jersey. She carries a clutch bag.

Ignoring the entreaties of a beggar woman at Ascot, two elegant racegoers continue on their way, 1923. Scarves decorate the dress of the woman in white and her companion demonstrates the fashion for bold tribal patterns, as seen on her skirt and sleeve.

A 1927 wedding joins members of the French and Italian royal families. The
bride's simple wedding dress is short and cut on the hip, following the style
of the day. A long train with scalloped or pearl-trimmed edges is typical of
1927 bridalwear, and the veil may have been pinned to the hair under wax
flowers. Dresses were often pale pink or cream.

Clarissa Churchill marries the future British Prime Minister Sir Anthony Eden in 1921. Head dresses were wired shape. Satin shoes and pearl detailing usually completed a bride's outfit.

A movie star marriage: Norma Shearer marries Irving Thalberg (they are fifth and sixth from the left), the associate executive of her studio, in October 1927. She has chosen romantic picture dresses with skirts of frothy tulle for her wedding. The uneven hem reflects the daywear trend of the late Twenties. Shearer was renowned for her smooth bias-cut dresses and sporty tennis whites.

Laurence Olivier, Adrianne Allen, Noël Coward and
Gertrude Lawrence in a scene from Coward's play
Private Lives, September 1930. Critics and theatregoers
were shocked by Coward's and Lawrence's animated
portrayal of a rowing couple who physically fought on
stage. Lawrence was renowned for her trouser suits in
this production designed by Edward Molyneux.

It may look as if she has just rolled up in her favourite carpet (above, left), but actually it is Greta Garbo in a white fur wrap, designed in New York for a night out at the theatre. Society girl Madame Lucien Lelong (née Princess Nathalie Paley), wife of the couturier (above, right) dresses for the evening. Her satin-lined wrap covers a longer line, more feminine, fitted dress, an example of the changing silhouette in the run-up to the Thirties.

Monkey fur trims on jackets and fox stoles, complete with head and tail, were popular for formal occasions and used to soften the edges of clothing. This theatre coat of 1925 by the House of Redfern (above, left) is trimmed with wolf fur. Unstructured wrap coats provided warmth for evening when worn over slip-like, beaded dance dresses. This one (above, right) is in fashionable black.

A black dress with swinging arm tassels by Paul Poiret (opposite). Poiret never regained his position in the fashion industry after he closed his house during the First World War. At the end of the Twenties he was declared bankrupt. Adele Astaire, dancer, actress and sister of Fred (above, left) wears a sleek 'little black dress', 1928. Josephine Baker (above, right) who shot to fame as a dancer and singer of *le jazz hot* in the Twenties, is dressed in a more theatrical little black dress. The fitted style suggests the picture was taken at the end of the decade.

Silent screen film siren Clara Bow, the 'It' girl, wears a long bias-cut silver lamé evening dress for her role in *No Limit* in 1931 (left). Lamé was a popular, glamorous choice for the evening and for film costumes. Noël Coward and Gertrude Lawrence in a scene from Coward's play, *Private Lives*, shown in London, September 1930 (opposite). Lawrence is remembered for the glamorous, white, bias-cut dress she wears here, designed by Edward Molyneux.

4 The Glamour Years

1930–1938

Joan Crawford, MGM film star, emerges from her dressing
room looking chic in shades and slacks. Major film stars
were required to look groomed and to live up to the
Hollywood dream both on and off screen. Fashionably full-
painted lips became known as a 'Joan Crawford mouth'.

4 The Glamour Years
1930–1938

Following the Wall Street Crash of 1929, unemployment soared and poverty spread. Many women retreated into the fairy-tale world of Fred Astaire and Ginger Rogers. The cheeky adolescent in her 'flapper' dress of the Twenties had matured into a sophisticated woman who yearned to emulate the silk-swathed stars of the silver screen.

Around the world, millions flocked to the talkies to see and (for the first time) to hear their idols, stars such as Marlene Dietrich, Joan Crawford, Greta Garbo and Jean Harlow. They became icons, idealised goddesses and arbiters of style. Image was all. In Hollywood, film studios hired costume designers to dress their stars both on and off screen: at Paramount Pictures, Travis Banton designed for Marlene Dietrich; Gilbert Adrian dressed Greta Garbo at MGM. Edith Head put Dorothy Lamour in a sarong and set a trend. Movie fans could dash from picture house to department store, where entire areas might be dedicated to selling copycat Hollywood looks. A host of would-be Letty Lyntons, Scarlett O'Haras and Mata Haris were soon parading their new styles on the street.

To carry off the Thirties style, women needed a movie star figure. The new bias-cut evening gowns, with their sinuous columns of flimsy fabric, revealed every bulge. The ideal figure was lithe, toned and streamlined, with thin hips, a defined waist and broad shoulders. Brassières were used not to flatten the bust but to lift and separate, and women wore bi-stretch Latex girdles to iron out any lumps and bumps. *Vogue* magazine commented on these long-line dresses in 1934: 'You'll look as thin as a reed and taller than ever, because of the long slip with its sudden flowering at the hem.' Diamanté clips and gold chokers glistened beside chiffon-topped black velvets, slippery white silk-satins, and gold lamé.

Thirties woman was spoilt for choice when it came to dressing. For daywear she might choose a slim-cut dress with wide shoulders and a belted waist, or perhaps a sharp, tailored suit which reached below the knee. Eveningwear fell into two main categories: the first was a classically draped, bias-cut style, perfected by Madeleine Vionnet. She was lauded for her halter neck gowns and simple wrap coats. The second harked back a generation to the prosperous *Belle Epoque*, with fitted bodices, bustle-style bows and sweeping skirts. In 1933 shoulders grew wide and exploded into leg-of-mutton and butterfly sleeves a year later. But a sleek, tailored evening suit in black was the really modern choice. 'Nothing in fashion is newer', said *Vogue* in 1935.

The very extravagant wore fur greatcoats that shadowed the long evening dresses. For everyone else, fur trims and wraps of all kinds were *de rigueur*. In a move inconceivable today, *Vogue* printed a chart of animal sketches to aid the shopper's choice of pelt. Squirrel or muskrat? Silver fox or Hudson seal?

As the decade passed, beach holidays and sunbathing became more fashionable. Holidaymakers donned sailor-style tops, shorts and thin floral dresses, and emulated Dietrich with matching mother-and-daughter swimwear.

Maverick designer Elsa Schiaparelli switched from philosophy to fashion design and brought a quirky edge to Parisian glamour. Following in Poiret's footsteps, her collaborations with avant-garde artists like Jean Cocteau and Salvador Dali created tall hats shaped like shoes and dresses with *trompe l'oeil* prints mimicking torn fabric. She built practical uplift brassières into dress bodices and exposed traditionally hidden zips as detailing.

But the clock was soon to strike twelve for a generation of Cinderellas dreaming of Hollywood. Hitler, Franco and Mussolini were busy carving up Europe. Very soon women would have to tighten their belts.

Wallis Simpson poses for the camera in 1936, before the abdication of King Edward VIII. Her day dress, probably made out of bias-cut silk, was designed to cling to the silhouette. Bold floral prints were fashionable during the Thirties. Mrs Simpson's favourite designer was the American Mainbocher. Her make-up and glossy, waved hair are stylishly perfect, in the manner of a Hollywood film star.

The Duchess of Kent with Prince Edward and Princess Alexandra leave for a holiday in 1937. The Duchess's spotted day dress sets off her two-tone, peep-toe shoes; these originated as beach shoes and became particularly popular in the 1930s. The Duchess carries a neat clutch bag.

An American couple pose at the Sands Point Horse Show in 1935 (left). The woman wears a simple day dress, which is belted to emphasise her waist. Hats were still worn outside the house, and hers has a fashionable slanted brim. (Opposite) The Duke and Duchess of Windsor at their house on the French Riviera in 1939. The Duchess's dress has the wide, voluminous sleeves that became fashionable during the late Thirties. The wide-shouldered, thin-hipped silhouette was the ideal for which women in the Thirties strived.

Female members of the Italian Fascist organisation (above) march in Tripoli, Libya, 1935. This picture shows the streamlined skirt shape, popular for daywear, with a slight pleat for easier movement. 'Blackshirts' (right) from Sir Oswald Mosley's British Union of Fascists, parade in Liverpool. Berets had become fashionable for daywear as well as for uniform.

Swedish actress Greta Garbo, who was famous for films such *Queen Christina* and *Ninotchka* with costumes designed by Adrian. Her hairstyle and her hats were widely copied. Here she wears a double-breasted wrap coat with a matching scarf collar.

Film star Marlene Dietrich and her husband Rudy Sieber walking in the streets of Paris in 1938. Dietrich was known for her mannish skirt suits with wide shoulders designed by Travis Banton, a style that would come back into fashion in the Eighties. Her look was notably urbane and sophisticated, and she often used furs as accessories.

Arch rivals 'Coco' Chanel (left) and her fellow designer Elsa Schiaparelli (opposite). The Thirties were Coco's heyday. She wears a Chanel suit (of course) but the lines are now sleeker, in the Thirties style. Schiaparelli, in her astrakhan-trimmed suit, was known for her sense of humour and the Surrealist references in her clothing. She helped to make the wide, shaped sleeve fashionable, and made eveningwear in tweed and pleated fabric to resemble bark.

Mannishly wide shoulders were popular, especially on jackets. This one is in white gabardine. Underneath she wears a brown linen shirt, with matching hat. During the Thirties, brown became an alternative basic dress colour to black.

English aviator Amy Johnson wears a woollen suit designed by Elsa Schiaparelli in 1936. The designer made her a complete collection of flying clothes. The newsprint scarf tied around her neck is a good example of Schiaparelli's quirky style; she also made matching newsprint bags and used fabric printed with music scores.

Marlene Dietrich shocked the more conservative with her mannish trouser suits and masculine hats worn on the side of the head, but the style quickly took off and copies soon appeared on the mass market.

A model poses in a Dietrich-style suit by Nicholl's in 1933, on a Regent Street roof in London. Dietrich was regarded as a style icon, and her on and off-screen clothes and image spawned a host of lookalikes. Even if women did not dare wear a wide-shouldered trouser suit, her hats, hair and make-up were noted and copied.

Elsa Schiaparelli brings culottes to London's Hyde Park in 1931 (left). This was the year she helped make beach overalls and jackets with broad shoulders fashionable. Schiaparelli had shot to fame when one of her first pieces, a black jumper with a *trompe l'oeil* bow, was spotted in a shop window by a department store buyer. Her companion wears fashionable gauntlet-style gloves. Culottes which could button back into a skirt were the practical choice for bicycling (opposite), and divided skirts were also worn for tennis in the same period.

Designers and the press bombarded women with clothing for The Season. These 1933 Ascot dresses are made by Dudeney. While the organdie dress on the left has matching gauntlet gloves in the same fabric, the one on the right has large, puffed sleeves, a style that became fashionable towards the end of the decade.

This Victor Stiebel dress of 1934 demonstrates the fascination with Victoriana, with its sweeping skirt clinging to the hips and then flaring outwards, the large bustle-style bow and the wide hat.

These long, romantic dresses could not be more different from the chemise dresses of the
Twenties, but have evolved from the *robes de style*. They were worn for The Season. Delicate
cotton became fashionable for dresses in America, and this wide-shouldered dress
(above, left) is set off by gossamer-thin gloves. The lace dress worn with a decorative parasol
(above, right) is in the *Belle Epoque* revival style with all its fuss and frills.

Even if your dress did not have wide, romantic shoulders, you could fake it by covering the shoulders with a short bolero (above, left). More lace-frilled skirts and a two-tiered cape (above, right) borrow from the styles of the early 1900s.

High-society fashion models, probably in America, show off their elegant little black dresses to wonderful effect. The white collars and cuffs and simple pearls or paste jewellery are inspired by Chanel.

Wide-shouldered coats were worn to emphasise the shoulder
line and the sleek lines of the dress underneath (above, left).
An ermine fur coat designed by Max (above, right) would
have been worn for the evening. The smartest were tailored
and fell to the ground with uneven hems.

The collars of this tailored coat by Schiaparelli are held together with a large button (above, left). Schiaparelli often used novelty buttons in the shape of swinging acrobats, beetles and womens faces. This 1934 double-breasted coat (above, right) is by the house of Jaeger; coats were often firmly wrapped and belted, contrasting with the flowing capes and evening wraps.

This neatly cut day dress of 1935, with its pencil skirt and pleated front, needs the large white bow to add a touch of Thirties glamour. Daywear was much less elaborate than the full-length dresses worn for evening, but it still required a neat figure as dresses and suits clung to the hips and waist.

Tailored suits were streamlined and practical for day. This one of 1935 is in chestnut and beige, in line with 1930s trend for brown as an alternative to black or grey. The extended lapels on the jacket emphasise the fashionably wide shoulders of the jacket.

(Opposite) These European jumpers with their graphic patterns would have been worn for casual daywear or resortwear, and are much more fitted than the loose jersey versions of the Twenties. Twinsets were popular and knitted cardigans were worn on top of day dresses. This jumper by Bruno Netti (right) has sharp shoulders, following the tailoring trends of the day.

Low-backed, white evening dresses were used to show off a deep tan. Film star Adrienne Ames (left) wears a dress with a classically draped back, which could possibly have been designed by Madeleine Vionnet or Alix Barton (later known as Madame Grès). Almost sci-fi-style wide sleeves made the column dresses worn for evening look slimmer and longer. This white jacket (opposite) by German designer Joe Strassner has pleated cap sleeves. Make-up, such as false eyelashes and lipstick, was worn boldly and eyebrows were plucked to oblivion.

Sleek, bias-cut dresses were worn for evening and formal occasions, and showed every curve, so girdles were used to slim down the hips. A model poses in a dress by Victor Stiebel (above, left), Hollywood actress Myrna Loy (above, centre) shows off the new erogenous zone, the back, and actress Gina Malo (above, right) wears a bejewelled Empire line gown.

Fashion editor-turned designer Mainbocher's black evening dress (above, left) sets off a diamanté feather at the waist. Velvet was still popular for evening and Chanel designed wide-shouldered evening suits in black velvet. This dress (above, centre) is by Robert Piguet who was known for his easy tailored dresses. Black satin trimmed with silver fox was used for this Mainbocher dress with its matching cape (above, right).

Judging by the suntans on show, this could be St Tropez, but it is not. It is Margate, on the Kent coast, where girls in a beach pyjama parade are disporting themselves in 1932 (right). Halter neck tops and low-backed swimming costumes were popular because of their tanning potential. The wrap 'modesty' skirts had been removed from bathing costumes, which now offered a sleeker silhouette for the beach. (Above) The sarong, too, became popular, thanks to Edith Head's designs for Dorothy Lamour in the film *The Jungle Princess*, 1936.

Actress Diana Wynyard in 1932. Trousers were worn as leisurewear, and they were almost always cut wide, revealing much less of the figure than the streamlined skirts and dresses of the era. Linen trousers were cut in a mannish style, with sharp pleats running down the front. These would have probably been worn for relaxed evenings on holiday or on the beach.

Although it is a little hard to believe, the relaxed Prince of Wales check woollen slacks and sharply tailored blue tweed jacket in this photograph were designed by Jacques Heim as beachwear. Heim had opened his own couture house in 1930 and produced beachwear and ranges specifically dedicated to a younger market. Draped bathing costumes, and even the bikini, were introduced by Heim.

Trousers were now deemed acceptable for beach and leisurewear and even for eveningwear. This outfit (above, left) is described as a 'summer play suit' and is probably an all-in-one suit. White was a popular colour, particularly to show off a suntan, and actress Gertrude Lawrence (above, right) makes full use of the effect in Monte Carlo.

Eleanor Stewart (above, left), winner of the MGM Voice and Talent Competition, wears matching sporty trousers and shirt, which could pass for daywear in the 1990s. Wide, sailor-style yachting pants, such as these worn by actress Joan Valerie (above, right), were made popular by Chanel. Underneath her cropped top she wears a halter neck top with ties at the waist.

Visitors dressed for the beach, with heavy suntans, admire the view of
Monte Carlo, August 1934. At that time the Riviera was a popular
destination for society's elite, and was still relatively unspoilt.

Getting away from it all. One way to escape all the glamour and guarantee fresh air and a suntan was to go hiking, a pastime that became very popular in the Thirties. Leisurewear styles were similar to beachwear and resortwear.

Some beach pyjamas were bright and often over the top, as in these versions (above), which even had matching hats. These girls (right) have decided to play bowls in their pyjamas, which are cut almost as wide as the Oxford bags worn by men in the 1920s. They differ from yachting pants in that they do not have sharp creases on the trouser legs.

Campers at Upshine, near Epping, on the outskirts of London, enjoy the summer
sun. They wear practical beach-style skirts with deep splits and side-button
fastenings over swimming costumes.

Picnicking girls near Richmond, on the River Thames near London, feel no need to cover their bodies from the sun. Their shorts and halter neck tops reveal a large expanse of flesh for maximum browning.

Marlene Dietrich (above and opposite, right) shows off clothing by Travis Banton, costume designer for Paramount Studios. Dietrich looks every inch the star with her high, pencilled eyebrows and smooth figure. Plastic surgery, enormous wardrobe budgets and lavish make-up ensured that films gave their audiences stars and fashions to aspire to. The most glamorous furs were tailored into jackets and coats (opposite, left) as in this gown from the film *Angel* (1937).

Fred Astaire and Ginger Rogers dance the night away in *Swing Time* in 1936. Rogers' dress, designed by Bernard Newman, is detailed with a row of tiny buttons down the front and a small sash, which makes references to turn-of-the-century dress.

Fred and Ginger in *Roberta* (1935), wearing costumes designed by Bernard Newman. The sleek, bias-cut dress is cut with a wider skirt for dancing, but more streamlined versions of this were typical eveningwear of the mid-Thirties. The dress serves as an effective backdrop for Ginger's diamanté jewellery.

Greta Garbo helped to revitalise the fashion for trench coats, and waterproofs were available from Barbour, Aquascutum and Burberry, just as the one shown (right). Made in beige gabardine, they often had matching waterproof hats. Paul Lukas and Rosalind Russell star in the detective film *The Casino Murder Case* (1935) (opposite), but it was Humphrey Bogart in the 1940s who is best remembered for gangsters, detectives and trench coat fashion.

Tailored suits were an important part of a woman's wardrobe in the 1930s. They now reached below the knee and were fitted so that they emphasised the waistline. Here Carole Lombard, a leading lady with Paramount Studios in Hollywood, poses in a suit topped with a fur bolero jacket.

Actress Bette Davis leaves a costume fitting for *Front Page Women* (1935). Tailored suits for the day were popular in wool and tweed. This suit is accessorised with a cheeky beret worn on the side of the head, a fashionable style of the day.

The white dress designed by Adrian and worn by Joan Crawford in the 1932 film *Letty Lynton* (left) had an enormous influence on fashion. Manufacturers copied it and women flocked to department stores to buy 'the Letty Lynton dress'. The dress also helped to kick-start the trend for wide shoulders. A woman wears a similar version in a heatwave on the promenade at Blackpool (above), and Joan Crawford (opposite) wears a softer version of the dress. The pom-pom frills of the sleeves have calmed down and now form a neat bolero shape.

Jean Harlow, in a scene from *Reckless*, wears a dress designed by Hollywood costumier Adrian. The film was made in 1935, but the minimal modern dress could easily belong to a woman in the mid-Nineties. Chanel had made black dresses fashionable, and throughout the century simple black styles have had a timeless appeal. In this era women still wore black dresses to show off their jewellery. Costume jewellery was widely worn, particularly Art Deco-style pieces in red, green and black paste.

Joan Crawford wears a more streamlined dress as Letty Lynton in 1932, again designed by Adrian. It demonstrates the fashion for classical drapery with its bias-cutting, draping and wrap details.

Softly draped bodices were used to frame the face and echo the soft waves of the hair. Push-up bras held the bust in place, and the bias-cutting emphasised rather than hid the bust-line (left). (Opposite) Constance Bennett and Clark Gable drink in *After Office Hours* in 1934. The smooth Empire line of her dress is emphasised by the fluid butterfly sleeves that form a wide curved line over the shoulders.

Draped neck lines and halter neck backs softened beachwear styles and moved them on for evening. Here Anna Sten, a Russian-born Hollywood actress, poses in a black dress topped with what is probably silver or gold lamé, which was popular for evening (along with silk, satin, chiffon, moiré and organie).

Actress Claudette Colbert, styled by Travis Banton, goes for a simpler draped-neck version in chaste white. Evening dresses were worn long and sweeping to the floor. Pearls were now more commonly worn around the wrist rather than the neck.

Joan Crawford in *No More Ladies* (1935) is dressed in a signature sleek and timeless dress by Adrian. The halter neck style was now important for eveningwear, and designer Madeleine Vionnet promoted the look. In the Thirties, costume jewellery was worn big and bold in the evening, in contrast with the demure, tailored looks and simple dresses for day.

Tailored suits were often cut sharp with exaggerated shoulders, and executed in tweed or wool. Designers known for their tailoring include American-based Hattie Carnegie, Irish designer Digby Morton and Paris-based designer Cristobal Balenciaga. Joan Crawford (right) in 1936 is wearing a belted suit with an exaggerated collar to emphasise the fashionable wide shoulders. Her off-screen wardrobe was designed by Hollywood costumier Adrian.

Joan Crawford poses in a sumptuous fur-trimmed dress. Diamanté clips were widely used to decorate simple black dresses, but here Crawfords glittering feathers are actually embroidered on the garment, and detailed with a hanging brooch.

Joan Crawford uses a different device to draw attention to the shoulders here, a short bolero ending in a wide bow. Bows were used on the backs and sides of dresses, and her waist is emphasised here with a large buckle. Sashes and belts with square buckles were popular waistline detailing for daywear.

Paul Sinclaire and his daughter relax in easy leisurewear at Easthampton, on Long Island. Her button-front pinafore dress is similar to Claire McCardell's dresses of the 1940s. The wide, capped sleeves were also translated into evening shapes at the time. The American market was already leading in mass-produced, ready-to-wear clothing.

Americans Mr and Mrs Jerome Napoleon Bonaparte show off their pooch at a Rhode Island dog show in 1934. Her smooth skirt may have been cut on the bias in silk, and elegantly clings to her figure; the outfit shows how the original shirtwaister and skirt from the beginning of the century have evolved. Her gauntlet gloves and two-tone shoes were at the height of fashion during the Thirties, and an Art Deco-style black and diamanté brooch sits at her throat.

The Duchess of Windsor in striped sequins stands on the right in the photograph.
Shoulder pads were fashionable; here the shoulders are restrained with a subtle leg-of-
mutton bulge where the sleeve meets the bodice on this sharp jacket. It probably covered
a long dress. The Duchess was very much a style icon and her clothing was followed
with interest. She wears a bracelet over her gloves, a style introduced by Chanel.

A woman dressed up in her evening clothes for a first night at the theatre in 1931. Her hair is trapped under a band in the style of the 1920s, but the draped silk or satin of her dress, topped with fur, are very much in a Thirties style. Evening bags were often ornate at this time, with sequinned purses and clutch bags in decorative leathers.

Lord and Lady Dufferin of Ava and Lady Rosslyn walk to the State Opening of Parliament in London in 1938 (opposite). The women wear sleek bias-cut dresses and fur boleros, a style also worn for eveningwear. (Right) Mrs Meade and Mrs McClure wait for the train to take them to Ascot races. American designer Mainbocher offered some particularly stylish printed dresses, such as the one worn on the right.

A woman tries to pick up a nutria by its tail at the fur-bearing animals exhibition in London. Furs were worn for evening and day; particularly popular were foxes with head, paws and tails all intact. Long-haired furs were preferred over short pelts.

Eccentric Phyllis Gordon takes her four-year-old pet cheetah from Kenya on a shopping spree in London in 1939. The animal seems less interested in 1930s retail therapy than its mistress. She wears a whole animal skin thrown over her shoulders, for at the time such a thing was regarded as a status symbol. For evening, furs were needed for warmth, especially if all that was fashionably permitted underneath was a long tube of silk.

The wedding of Laurence Olivier and Jill Esmond Moore, Olivier's first wife, in 1930.
Her romantic dress with its neat, circular neckline is elegant and simple compared
with the fussy Victorian-style dress of the woman on the left.

The Duke of Windsor marries Mrs Simpson in 1937. Her blue crepe wedding dress and trousseau were made by Mainbocher, who, after working as editor-in-chief at French *Vogue*, went on to open a successful couture house in Paris. The elegant cut of her jacket with its ruched panel, ending on an Empire line seam, was mimicked for the daywear of the late Thirties. Her headdress would have been wired to stay up, and is reminiscent of the Twenties bridal fashions.

Crisis at the wedding of Lady Honor Guinness in 1933 as her veil is caught by
the wind. This sleek, bias-cut dress with its draped neck line is similar to the
eveningwear styles of the time.

The wedding of British film star Marjorie Hume takes place in the same year, and she wears a dress with a similarly draped neck line. Her dress is plain, but detailing at the time included pearl-studded skullcaps, silk flowers worn in the hair, pearl-edged bodices and neck lines with wreaths of cut-out leather leaves.

This woman waiting for the Ascot train at Waterloo Station in 1936 is wearing a jacket with the wide, soft leg-of-mutton sleeves that came into fashion, and were particularly used on evening-wear and formal-wear pieces.

The frothy frills of these racegoers contrast with the sleek lines of a bias-cut dress. Large necklaces or neckpieces were worn and gilded leaves were particularly popular for the evening. There was a move away from the ropes of swinging pearls and beads of the Twenties.

The bias-cut skirts of the Thirties were designed to flatter the figure, and the designer Edward Molyneux was particularly popular for his clean, smooth lines and simple, elegant pieces. Queen Elizabeth (above) in 1937 wears a long, flattering skirt. (Opposite) Marina, Duchess of Kent (on the right), wears an equally elegant streamlined suit with a casual over-jacket, possibly made of crepe. A top-heavy fur wrap or wide hat emphasised the slimness of the skirt and hips. The Princesses Elizabeth and Margaret, in matching outfits, need attention.

Greta Garbo (opposite) was the Hollywood star who had the biggest influence on hat trends. She started a trend for berets by wearing them in *The Kiss* (1929), she wore jewelled skullcaps in *Mata Hari* (1931) (bottom, left) and pill boxes in *The Painted Veil*. Schiaparelli designed tall hats, inspired by a surrealist shoe placed on the head (centre, left) and the Marina hat was named after the Duchess of Kent (centre, right). Hats that came down over one eye were fashionable. Joan Crawford wears one in *Letty Lynton* (1932) (bottom, right) and Norma Shearer wears a similar style (top, right). Marlene Dietrich helped to pioneer a man's-style hat. A similar version is seen here worn by Joan Crawford (top, left).

Shorts were now beachwear essentials and were usually worn with short, white ankle socks, as shown by actress Carole Lombard (left); Lombard was renowned for her coarse language and for throwing lavish parties. Nautical themes were also popular and can be seen on the sailor-front detailing of Lombard's shorts, and on the striped nautical-style top (right). The house of Worth, which was still going, designed nautical resortwear with striped tops, berets and blazers.

Sunglasses, particularly those with white or tortoiseshell rims, were the fashionable new accessories for the beach. Model Marcella Flood wears hers on Long Island in 1937. Other accessories include rubber beach hats and pointed, flat, rubber beach shoes and wide sun hats with waved brims.

On the beach these girls show the new androgynous style of bathing costume. The skirt has been removed, leaving a smooth and simple line. Stretch-rayon and cotton were used for costumes, and bright colours such as red, yellow and green were fashionable.

Members of the Hitler Youth get their dose of fresh air in 1938. Group exercise in the open air was very much a fad of the era. Health and sport had become an integral part of fashionable life. The exerciser had the added bonus of getting a suntan and losing a few pounds so as to be able to get into that bias-cut dress.

Dancer and 'physical culture' expert
Rosemary Andrée tests a new type of
exercising apparatus in 1935. Foam baths,
which were said to induce weight loss, and
electric treatments were also used.

Picnickers in a London park wear revealing swimming costumes with cut-out holes for getting a tan, although the result must have been two unsightly brown spots. Costumes were now elasticised and could hold their shape when wet, allowing women to look elegant when emerging from the water after a swim.

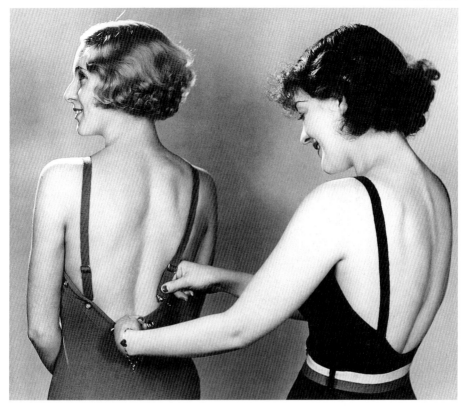

Swimming costumes with removable straps for sunbathing were a popular alternative to halter neck costumes. Fashionable evening dresses often sported low-cut backs, and these demanded smooth skin and an even tan. Sporty belts were used as detailing on swimming costumes, often with circular buckles, and coloured rubber shoes were worn for the beach.

Mae West was known for her curves and influenced the shape of Elsa Schiaparelli's perfume bottle. She was also arrested on obscenity charges when she appeared in her play *Sex*. Ostrich feathers were used by Hollywood to trim luxurious glamour gowns, such as this one.

Film star Carole Lombard relaxes at home. The wide, kimono-style sleeves of her dress were part of a trend for Eastern drapery, pioneered by designer Madame Grès, who borrowed references from the wrapped and draped Indian dhotis and saris. Other designers used bamboo buttons, mandarin collars and Japanese-style obi sashes as detailing.

Glamorous bedroom-wear, such as wraps and long, bias-cut dresses, fulfilled the role of the tea-gown. Today many of these pieces appear to be no different from eveningwear. Tallulah Bankhead (opposite, above) is photographed in the London stage play *Let Us Be Gay* (1930), Vivien Leigh lounges at home (opposite, bellow) and Jean Harlow goes for full glamour in a white sequinned negligée (right) in *Dinner at Eight* (1933), designed by Adrian.

Janet Allen, a professional dancing partner at Streatham Dance Hall in south
London, has breakfast in bed in a stylish dressing gown, full make-up and nail
varnish. False nails and a fully lipsticked mouth were trends of the era.

These 'Cosy-leg' pyjamas 'that won't ride up' were from 1936, and were probably designed for wearing in bed and as loungewear, but dresses and negligées were preferred at the time.

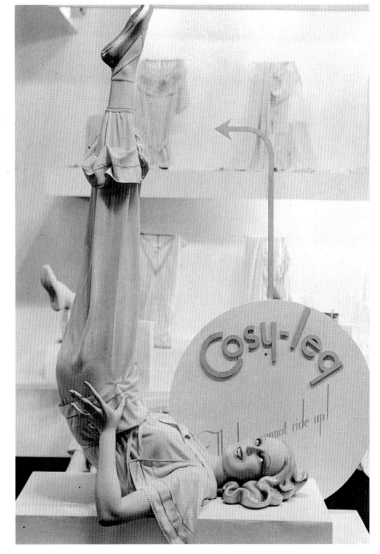

This corselet uplifts the bust and smoothes the torso and hips, and the petticoats would add body to the skirts of a romantic Ascot dress. The photograph was touched up to make the model look slimmer, which is partly why she looks as if she is floating.

Model Jean Seaton in the latest underwear, a lace-edged silk cami-shift from 1938 that would have been worn under a daywear suit. Pants or briefs, initially regarded as unattractive, were being worn at the end of the Thirties.

Women at work in a corset factory in 1939, fitting the corsets onto dummies.
Women still wore body-controlling underwear, but it had become feather-light
compared to the whalebone stays of thirty years earlier. More feminine underwear
included silk cami-knickers, ruched tops and light slips inserted with lace or
embroidered with flowers. Push-up bras helped to emphasise the bust.

In 1938 a woman reveals how she manages to look so sleek in a long, bias-cut dress. Her all-in-one stretch corselet was designed to hold in the hips and waist, and would have been made out of elasticised cotton-satin. Flesh-coloured silk stockings were fastened to suspenders, and corselets often had low backs that could work with evening styles.

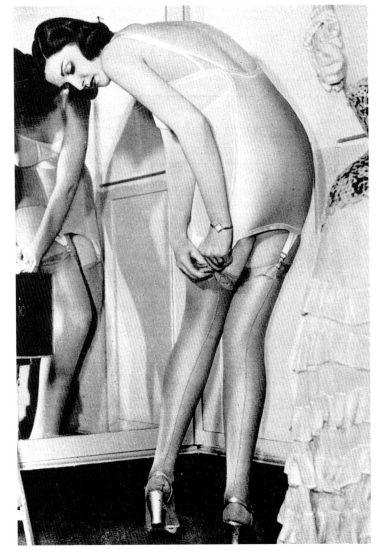

Hair fashions were soft and feminine compared with the previous decade. Greta Garbo (top, left) shows the long, waved romantic style. She was also known for her bobbed hair. Claudette Colbert's fringe was widely copied (top, right) and Carole Lombard (bottom, left) shows the highly stylised waves that were so popular. Revue star Frances Day (bottom, right) shows a more tousled, thicker style. The craze for neo-Victorian styles brought about a trend for flower-topped chignons and decorated hair combs.

Jean Harlow started the craze for peroxide blonde hair when she dyed hers for the film *Hell's Angels* in 1930; she even starred in another film called *Platinum Blonde* (1931). Blonde hair helped to set off the fashionable white evening dresses popular at the time. Harlow's fans would never see her grow old: she died of kidney failure aged only twenty-six.

5 Make Do and Mend

1939–1946

During the Second World War even stars had to climb down from their pedestals and muck in with the rest. Here actress Margaret Vyner bundles her hair into a scarf, ready to do the housework, 1941. At the end of the war Jacqmar advertised its Victory scarves in *Vogue* and this scarf is probably printed with morale-boosting slogans, scattered amongst the V for Victory motifs.

5 Make Do and Mend
1939–1946

In Britain, as the State took control of the wartime purse strings, rationing enforced an era of compulsory minimalism. The lavish film star look of the Thirties was now viewed as flashy, unpatriotic and vulgar. In 1943 *Vogue* warned: 'You'll have fewer clothes because you have not the time, money or coupons to clutter up your life with non-essentials… You'll have simpler clothes because in these days anything elaborate looks silly.' Restriction orders outlawed wasteful cutting and excess trimmings, rationed limited consumerism and the Utility scheme offered Government-approved clothing at fixed prices. Luxurious fabrics like silk and nylon (introduced in 1938) were commandeered for parachutes, golf balls became gas masks and mattresses became life jackets. Fabrics such as rayon, viscose and even (illicitly) blackout material were left for making clothes.

On both sides of the Atlantic top designers were called up to do their bit. The British Board of Trade drafted in a group which included Hardy Amies, Victor Stiebel and Edward Molyneux to design a complete civilian 'Utility' wardrobe to be mass-produced and bought with clothing coupons. *Vogue* backed the move, saying that there was 'an overwhelming case, in mass production, for starting with superlative design'. Norman Hartnell made clever, practical uniforms for Girl Guides helping with post-war relief work. Their grey-green tweed dresses had long sleeves that could be buttoned on and off. Wide ski trousers were tucked into boots and teamed with long-sleeved, tight jumpers. The Women's Voluntary Service had Digby Morton to thank for their uniforms and in the United States. Mainbocher designed elegant clothes for the Women Accepted for Voluntary Emergency Service. Couturiers were learning how to work with manufacturers, an important development in view of the ready-to-wear designer boom that was to come after the war.

As the men fought overseas, women rolled up their sleeves and knuckled down to work. The Land Girls pulled on their corduroy breeches as they dug for victory. Women's daywear was sharp and to the point, with heavy shoes (often with wooden soles to save on leather), sharp-shouldered jackets and knee-length skirts. As the war continued, women devised a new mix-and-match formula to stretch their wardrobes. Suits gave way to contrasting shirts and skirts. British *Vogue* patriotically focused on DIY fashion and 'Make Do and Mend'. It advised sewing different coloured ribbons into pleats of skirts, embellishing black dresses with paisley pockets and turning maternity capes into reefer jackets. White collars and cuffs were used to economise on fabric, and berets, hairnets and turbans replaced hats when straw ran out. Meanwhile, isolated by the German occupation, Paris had lost its influence. Coco Chanel and Madeleine Vionnet shut up shop; Edward Molyneux, Charles Creed, Mainbocher and Charles James all fled abroad. Those who remained worked in a bubble, surviving by producing lavish costumes for the Nazis' women. But even couturiers had to watch their step: when Madame Grès draped her models in the patriotic red, white and blue of the French tricolour the Germans immediately closed her house down.

In America, designers such as Vera Maxwell and Alice Evans were putting women in sporty leisurewear. Claire McCardell teamed up with manufacturers Townley Frocks to offer simple, ready-to-wear separates in jersey, denim, ticking and calico. Her wrap-style dresses, jersey bodysuits and fabric-covered ballet-style shoes appealed to women because they were simple but well designed. By 1944 American styles included the jumper dress, this time round with sharp shoulders, wide-shouldered pinafores and shoulder bags like drawstring rucksacks. More glamorous were voluminous evening gowns and sci-fi-look padded white satin jackets by Charles James. On a visit to New York in 1945 the photographer Cecil Beaton was stunned by the 'wonderful young women with their towering Marie Antoinette hair-do's… It was as if the war had never happened.'

The war in Europe finally over, Paris needed to prove that it was still leader of the pack. Facing severe fabric shortages, necessity nonetheless proved the mother of invention. Ingeniously, 237 wire mannequins wearing scaled-down versions of the couture collections were exhibited in miniature stage sets at the Louvre. Each mannequin was just 70 centimetres high and fully dressed in couture clothing, from underwear to accessories. The *Théâtre de la Mode* toured the world, putting Paris back on the map. And couture was back in business with a new designer up its sleeve.

In 1940s London this chic woman uses flowers and ribbon detailing on her pockets to jazz up her sharp jacket, which she may have customised herself. Until now the skirt and jacket of a suit had usually been made to match. During the war, however, more versatile mix-and-match separates were worn to stretch the wardrobe.

Two Bond Street shoppers, wearing elegant suits and what appear to be real stockings, carry their gas masks slung over the shoulder in cardboard boxes on strings in the first months of war. Later on, fashions adapted to include special gas mask shoulder bags that were made to match a particular outfit and larger, hand-held leather bags, such as the one shown here.

Journalist Anne Scott James wears a men's-style trouser suit in 1941. Women started to wear 'slack suits' for relaxing at home or for 'manual' work. Anne Scott James was to sit on the committee for fashion and accessories of the 'Britain Can Make It' exhibition after the war, which aimed to promote British products for export and to regenerate trade.

Private Hardy Amies puts the finishing touches to Lachasse's 1940 Spring collection before returning for duty in an officer cadet training unit. Amies became designer and managing director of Lachasse, which specialised in women's tweed suits. Even though this picture was taken in January 1940, before rationing and clothing restrictions were introduced, skirts were cut shorter and dresses were nipped in at the waist in the wartime 'waste not' style.

Models pose outside designer Edward Molyneux's London offices in 1941(left). This hooded tweed coat (above) was designed in 1939, when designers were still able to use ample lengths of fabric for their designs. Designer Robert Piguet designed similar hooded shelter coats.

Two women pose in their 'siren suits'; these were demure wool dressing gowns, which were warmer and more suitable than Thirties-style negligees for running out to the air raid shelter at a moment's notice. Digby Morton was known for his siren suit designs. The picture is dated 1939, the year designers reacted to the crisis by designing gas mask-size bags and jersey turbans for night-time air raid elegance.

The women left behind could always keep the men close to their hearts with nightwear pyjamas embroidered with a Royal Air Force emblem. Silk was ruled out for civilian clothing in Britain; these pyjamas may well have been made of rayon, the wartime substitute.

Posing at a picnic (left), these girls model American-style cotton casual dresses influenced by workwear styles. The navy and white striped dress on the left conforms to Utility regulations and would have been sold at a controlled price. The girl in the middle wears a dress with a detachable bib top to keep her white shirt clean. Colours for American-style dresses were bold, and white, because it got dirty so easily, was usually kept for shirts, collars and cuffs.

Well-made American practical, ready-to-wear fashion was
the envy of Europe. Here American-style dungarees have a
detachable apron that can be washed and ironed
separately. America continued to develop versatility and
comfort in clothing until the end of the century.

This bright blue pinafore was worn over a striped shirt (above, left). These workwear separates were made from cotton or linen which, compared with 'fancy' dress fabrics, were easily washable. An all-in-one boiler suit had large pockets and harem-style trouser bottoms for practical gardening (above, right), a style brought back by Claire McCardell. These American designs were made up in Britain and sold at Bourne & Hollingsworth on Oxford Street, as imports were forbidden.

Small prints that could be easily matched on a seam were used for formal summer day dresses to restrict fabric wastage (left and above), and adding white collars and cuffs saved precious dress material. The matching dresses (opposite) would have used up seven precious coupons each.

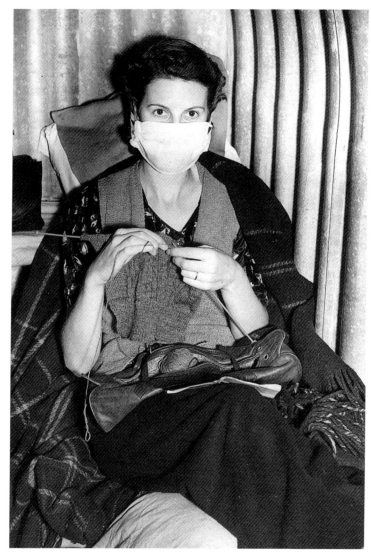

Clickety-click went the wartime knitting needles, as women and children knitted for Victory. This woman knitting in an air raid shelter (left) wears a gauze mask, which the diseased or cold-ridden were advised to wear to reduce the risk of spreading infection in the confined space of a shelter. Women knit socks for the forces (opposite, above), and children knit shawls for themselves, to wear in the bomb shelters at school (opposite, below). Knitwear became very fashionable in the 1950s, possibly as a result of the wartime enthusiasm for knitting.

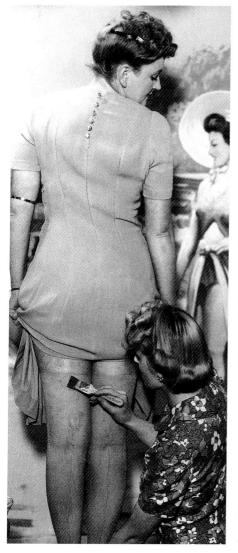

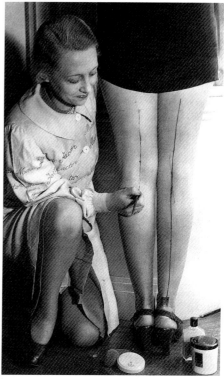

Just like in the Twenties the shorter skirt showed off the legs, but in Britain sheer stockings in silk, or much sought after nylon, were in short supply. Women turned to wool stockings in winter and tried *trompe l'oeil* stockings for summer. Here a beautician applies tanning lotion in the Bare Leg Beauty Bar in Croydon, south London (left), in front of a beach scene backdrop and a Max Factor beautician paints on the stocking seams (above). Women even used cocoa or gravy.

Women fight for coupon-free, sub-standard artificial stockings in a flash sale. In 1941 British civilian women were allocated sixty-six coupons per year for their complete wardrobe. A single pair of stockings alone would use up two whole precious coupons.

Queen Elizabeth talks to a group of bombed-out south
Londoners in 1940. As the daywear silhouette grew
slimmer and shorter, hats got bigger – they were not
rationed. The woman in the pinstriped suit wears
another fashion that was fuelled by wartime necessity:
bags with shoulder straps were much more practical
than hand-held bags.

A day at the races, France, 1945. This woman's lavish fur stole, neat hat and decadently opulent high-heeled boots bring to life what would have otherwise been a very plain dress.

These two crepe dresses conform to British Utility fabric and price standards, but are both elegant and roomy. Taken in 1946, this picture shows how the new feminine silhouette with its wider skirt had replaced the pinched, mean and slim war look.

American actress Carole Landis marries Thomas Wallace in London in 1943. If she had been British, her dress would have been made from rayon or viscose, but in America more luxurious fabrics were available; this would have been silk or even nylon. Her guests wear bold make-up. During the war many of the ingredients that went into make-up were scarce. Rich lipstick, an absolute essential for the fashion-conscious woman, was crumbly and the results were often blotchy.

Nell Dearing of the Express Dairy cuts her wedding cake. Her headdress has a very short, scarf-like veil, probably as a result of the fabric shortages of the time. Women wore both knee-length and long dresses to get married in, and the fashionable colours were pale pink and pale blue as well as white or cream.

The 'Forces' Sweetheart', singer Vera Lynn, shows off the wartime silhouette in 1942 with its sharp shoulders and close-fitting dresses. Day dresses were cut in linen or rayon, and coats and suits in wool. Fur was still popular for jackets, mufflers, boleros and stoles. In this photograph Vera Lynn is carrying an entire fox.

Actress and comedienne Gracie Fields poses with a bashful soldier in Rome. In 1945, the year this picture was taken, civilian women were wearing felt berets with coloured bands similar to the one sported by 'Our Gracie' here.

For day, dresses sported military belt detailing and buttons; this one (above, left) has a detachable top which can be combined with another skirt, 1946. Sharply cut little black dresses were sometimes decorated with white collars and cuffs, as this home-made one (above, centre), 1941. Fly-front, button-through dresses could be worn on their own, or open as a coat over another dress for a more versatile look (above, right), 1946.

This afternoon dress in bright green, by Jacques Heim, 1946 (above, left), has a detachable front panel. Pairs of old dresses were recycled so that the dress on top could be worn open from neck to knee, the gap being filled with panels from the second dress. This chic 1941 dress with military-style buttoned pocket detailing (above, right) is by Edward Molyneux, who was based in London during the war. He also designed Utility scheme prototypes.

In Britain in 1942, a clutch of top designers were asked to come up with Utility designs in line with cutting, fabric and price restrictions, to sell on to manufacturers. (Above) An original, on the left, is worn next to its mass-produced copy. Norman Hartnell provided prototypes (opposite, right) for the Utility scheme, and this two-tone dress (opposite, left) was also made to Utility specifications.

The skirt of this dirndl-style summer skirt was successfully made from three yards of bright red, green and black remnant curtain material. Wide-printed skirts such as these were popular for beachwear, 1946.

Under the 'Make and Mend' initiative of 1942 run by women's organis-ations, women were shown ingenious methods of patching together old clothes to make new garments. The results are impress-ive, but lack the elegance that was so carefully preserved by many women of the war era.

In true 'make-do-and-mend' fashion, this women has thriftily tailored an elegant 1941 coat from a white candlewick bedspread, as recommended in *Picture Post*. In the same year 'tailor-knit' jackets, with a similar looped wool finish, appeared in *Vogue* and were proclaimed the height of elegance.

Paris couture survived Hitler's plans to move its houses to Berlin and Vienna, but was still criticised by some for pandering to its Nazi patrons during the war. This woollen coat by Cristobal Balenciaga of autumn 1945 shows the evolution of a more curvy, post-war silhouette, with its defined waist and abundant use of fabric at the shoulders. Two years later fully-fledged feminine fashion was to be flung into the spotlight with Christian Dior's new look.

The Croydon store Kennards, in south London, organises an open-air fashion show in 1943 to display the latest Utility clothing worn with artificial silk stockings. Utility meant clothes which conformed to cloth standards approved by the Government. It had distinctive buttons bearing the logo CC41, and the pieces were regarded as desirable and of good quality.

These British Land Army girls of 1940 (opposite) in their dungarees were among approximately 80,000 women who enrolled to work on the land during the war. They also wore breeches. Italian partisans associated with the *Partito d'Azione* have joined up to liberate their country from German occupation (above). They wear trench coat-style overcoats, similar to styles worn by soldiers in the First World War, and sturdy shoes.

A woman takes her high heels to a post-war Berlin 'swop shop' to exchange them for more practical winter shoes. Chunky cork and wooden soles were used for day, and raffia and canvas were substituted when leather was redirected from civilian use to make army boots. Synthetic materials were also used to make shoes and galoshes.

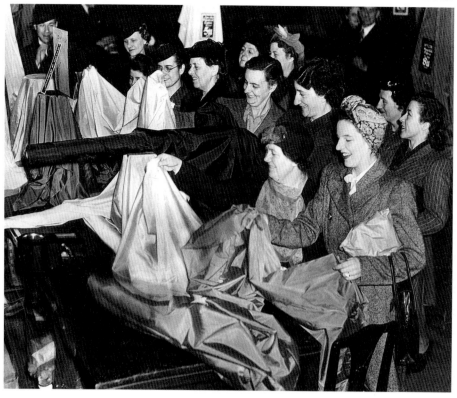

Women shoppers cannot believe their luck after stumbling upon this
Government surplus parachute nylon in 1945. The down side is
that nylon costs two clothing coupons per yard. Nylon was seen as
the unobtainable wonder-fabric, and was used for making
parachutes rather than for civilian use.

Josephine Baker gives the troops a Victory song at a party in 1945. During the war she also worked for the Red Cross and the French Resistance and was awarded the *Croix de Guerre*, the *Rosette de la Résistance* and was appointed to the *Légion d'Honneur* for her efforts. Her dress is similar to bridalwear and eveningwear styles worn before the war but may well have been a modern dress by Madame Grès or Maggie Rouff.

Marlene Dietrich returns home to New York in 1945 in uniform. She made over five hundred appearances in front of American troops overseas and gave propaganda broadcasts in German, for which she was awarded the US Medal of Freedom.

A Parisian model shows off her cripplingly high wedge shoes which have soles made of wood, September 1944. Designer Salvatore Ferragamo had introduced platform shoes before the start of the war, and went on to experiment with shoes made from snail shells, webbing, lace and nylon. Platform shoes were to come back into fashion in the Seventies.

Three American GIs stationed in Germany after the war
steadfastly ignore a pair of German girls. 'Fraternisation'
was banned. The girl on the left wears platform shoes,
with soles possibly made of wood or cork, and a
lightweight summer coat over her dress.

In 1945 the *Théâtre de la Mode* brought Paris couture in miniature to London in an attempt to revitalise the French fashion industry after the war. Here girls in uniform admire the decadently wide skirts, which were soon to become mainstream fashion. The clothing was presented in lit 'theatres', and both Jean Cocteau and the painter Christian Bérard contributed to the project.

Members of the American Women's Auxiliary Corps test perfumes in
Paris at the end of the war. Their uniforms were designed by Philip
Mangone. American troops queued outside the Chanel boutique after
the liberation of Paris, to buy some of the much sought after Chanel
No. 5 scent for their girls back home.

This Miami Beach style of 1946 shows American women in their mass-produced trousers and tops. The girl on the left wears a pinafore-style top over a striped shirt, a style that was also popular for pinafore dresses. Her hair is worn in the fashionable doughnut-shaped bun. The white shirt worn by the girl third from left is an example of the American trend for Latino-style wide skirts worn with puffed sleeve tops.

During the war, much of the wool available had been reserved for uniforms, but these 1946 woollen civilian outfits by Daks in sober grey or bracken were also accompanied by woollen dinner gowns and woollen evening coats. The casual trousers and shirts ape military styles with button-up pockets and wide trousers.

Hats started out large at the beginning of the war. As materials such as straw ran out, women improvised with precious scraps of dress material to make miniature doll-like hats which were worn perched on the head (opposite), like the feathered head-band worn by actress Phyllis Calvert (opposite, top middle). Berets, turbans, hairnets and snoods (right) were also adopted as cheaper alternatives and customisation was encouraged. The dove motif, a symbol of peace, is used to decorate a victory hat of 1945 (opposite, middle right).

Ingrid Bergman in a scene from the film *Casablanca* (1942). Her relaxed dress with pinafore detailing over a resort-style striped top is a fine example of the way the American sports style made its way into daywear dresses. She is wearing peep-toe shoes that in Britain were frowned upon as dangerous for war work and regarded as unnecessarily extravagant.

Actress Lauren Bacall in provocative pose. While the British painted on their stockings and ate rehydrated eggs, American women were wearing nylons and peeling oranges. Bacall's nipped-in waist and wide skirt was a look that only caught on in Europe after the war. Her black polo neck top anticipates the beatnik style which emerged in the mid-Fifties.

Relaxing on the beach in Blackpool in 1942. Younger girls reacted to the stocking shortage by wearing short ankle socks rather than painting on their stockings. Beach styles of the time included wide-printed, cotton knee-length skirts (for those who could afford the luxury), matching wide-brimmed hats and knitted cotton T-shirts.

Girls show their legs at the fair, riding on the caterpillar in Southend in 1945. The girl on the left appears to have tucked her wide-legged knickers into the bottom of her stretch girdle (worn underneath) in anticipation of the windy ride. Has she let her skirt fly up on purpose?

This American wrap-around 'play dress' was probably made out of stretch cotton trimmed with lace, and was worn with matching shorts underneath.

The bikini was launched in France by designers Jacques Heim and Louis Réard in 1946, and took off in a big way in Europe during the 1950s. One-piece swimming costumes were also still fashionable.

Stripes and seashell prints livened up a streamlined, one-piece swimming costume. Halter necks were still popular, and on the beach women wore open-toed canvas shoes with ballet-style ribbons which wrapped around the ankle.

Two women smoke, pose and worry about their hair by the side of the pool at Roehampton, London, in 1943. The more revealing bikini was not popular yet, but bra tops in rayon worn with short skirts like this one were already fashionable. The women wear full make-up and hair, regarded as the hats of the period, was worn towering and full.

Swansea girls take tea in the 1939 sunshine wearing fashionable white-rimmed sunglasses. Knitted cotton matching shorts and tops were worn as leisurewear and white versions were worn for tennis. When dress fabric was scarce, terry cloth, canvas and curtains were used to make sports and leisurewear.

Pre-shrunk cotton or rayon was used often used for beach and leisurewear. These shorts (right) are in red and the Viyella shirt is decorated with green checks. Girls relax by the river in 1941 (above). The swimming costume is probably made out of elasticised cotton and may also have featured ruched detailing at the hem.

In April 1939 *Picture Post* reported on the diversity of the Paris collections, suggesting that 'it's because we're all so unsettled in our minds that we can't decide on one definite line'. By September war had been declared. This scarlet satin coat worn over a hooped lace skirt is by Balenciaga, its Thirties bodice giving way to an 18th-century-style gown. Paris was to continue producing lavish clothes throughout the war.

Outside Paris, evening dresses were cut slim and long. In 1940 Molyneux's dress (above, left) is still opulent, with a jewelled neck line and an extravagant use of fabric for the puffed sleeves. (Above, centre) By 1945, separates had been introduced for evening. This lamé top is combined with a long black skirt, with a slit to the knee. (Above right) By 1942, flared skirts, fur trims, net dresses and tiered skirts were forbidden and long gloves and jewelled clips were no longer being made. This 'Austerity' peg-top dress in crepe was about as formal as it got.

Many women copied the softly waved 'peekaboo' hairstyle of actress Veronica Lake, with one lock of hair falling over the eye. Eventually she was asked to cut her hair, as the copycat styles were causing accidents in factories when the workers' long tresses became caught up in machinery. Here Veronica Lake wears full Hollywood glamour make-up, but European women had to make do with shoe polish for their eyebrows, red wine instead of rouge and buffing their nails rather than painting them.

Hair was worn high up on the head, and it grew higher as hat materials grew scarcer. Doughnut buns and chignons were popular and hair was often curled into high headdresses (above, left and right). Actress Betty Grable wears her hair in high curls (top, left) and actress Jean Gillie (top, right) goes for a longer curled style, which retains height on top of the head.

As clothing materials grew scarce women placed more emphasis on their hair and make-up. Here women prepare for a night's dancing in 1939. Their long hair has been carefully rolled, curled and pinned.

6 New World—New Look
1947–1956

A model wearing a New Look dress in the style of Christian Dior's 1947 collection is seized by two furious women in the rue Lepic, Paris. Both are still dressed in streamlined, wartime clothes. The lavish use of fabric for the new, full-skirted dresses was criticised by some women as being both unpatriotic and extravagant. They picketed the house of Dior, but the resulting publicity only fuelled the enthusiasm for the wide-skirted trend.

6 New World–New Look
1947–1956

With fewer wartime constraints, fashion began to blossom. In 1945 designers smoothed off fashion's sharp lines to create a softer silhouette, but it was Christian Dior who had the nerve to exaggerate the feminine silhouette to cartoon-like proportions. With the provocative swish of a wide skirt, Dior brought fantasy to life with his first ever Paris couture collection of 1947. Women were scandalised but thrilled by the fairy-tale extravagance of ballerina skirts, tapered waists and bust-enhancing bodices. Dior thumbed his nose at the post-war poverty and lack of materials, using as much as twenty-five yards of fabric for a single dress. Governments condemned it and American protest groups denounced it, but it was too late. Forget unpatriotic, impractical, expensive: women had already fallen in love with the romantic style which made the wartime suits look so mean, even if wearing a Dior dress meant a return to the corsets and hip pads of the *Belle Epoque*. In 1947 *Picture Post* commented: 'The shirt-waists and full skirts of the Nineties are fashion news today.' Carmel Snow called it the 'New Look', and Dior was launched.

Christian Dior had been singled out for attention by the textile giant Marcel Boussac, who offered to fund the opening of his couture house. Boussac would not be disappointed in his choice. The young visionary had soon built his own name into an aspirational brand. Just as Gucci would in the 1990s, Dior set the trends, everyone else copied them and the company reaped the considerable financial rewards. He tempted his couture customers with newer looks each season: the H-line, the A-line, the tulip line and the Y-line. By 1954 he was presiding over an empire, with boutiques, ready-to-wear, scent, stockings, accessories and lingerie running alongside his couture line.

If Dior was a pedlar of dreams, Cristobal Balenciaga was a fashion purist, offering sculptural drapery and sophisticated tailoring. His ergonomic suits with stand-away collars were smooth, and, in contrast to wide New Look skirts, he offered tight pencil skirts with jackets that rested on the hip.

While women were squeezing themselves into waspie corsets and stilettos, Coco Chanel, now over seventy, came stalking back with her relaxed suits and comfortable, unrestrictive dressing.

With the increase of ready-to-wear and mass production, couture found itself being shunted onto the sidelines. From the early days of the century couturiers had sold *toiles*, or couture samples, to manufacturers so that they could reproduce and sell copies of the couture looks with the couturiers' permission. During the 1930s Depression, America severely taxed imported couture originals but imposed no such taxes on *toiles*. The American mass production of copies from Paris increased markedly. During the war America had proved that ready-to-wear could work without Paris's design influence, and that the rich would buy well-designed, off-the-peg clothes if they were offered in a wide enough range of sizes. America began to lead in quality, mass-produced, ready-to-wear clothing.

In the Twenties, European designers such as Jean Patou had launched leisure ranges to run alongside their couture businesses and in the 1930s couturier Lucien Lelong launched a line of dresses that were ready-made rather than individually fitted to a woman's figure. After the war Jacques Fath, Hardy Amies, Christian Dior and others soon followed, launching their own ready-to-wear lines; they often teamed up with manufacturers to take care of the production but designed the clothes themselves. Women could now buy into a designer brand 'off the peg' at a reduced price. Next, European designers started to skip the couture route altogether, with Chloé, Emilio Pucci and Albert Lempereur all launching up-market, well-designed, ready-to-wear clothes.

The Fifties marked the liberation of the teenager as free spirit. A rash of subcultures was spawned: biker girls rode up behind the boys in unisex jeans, boots and leather jackets and beatnik girls danced to be-bop in head-to-toe black. Manufacturers spotted a gap in the market and quickly bridged it, designing reasonably priced, fashionable clothes specifically targeted at the young.

Christian Dior's first ever couture collection in 1947 was to change the way women looked for the next decade. The sheer amount of fabric used caused outrage. This famous Bar suit, with its nipped-in jacket, sloped shoulders and sweeping skirt, epitomised his New Look silhouette. Flying saucer hats and stiletto heels were the necessary accessories.

This dress by Ronald Paterson in 1955 is heavily influenced by Dior. Shorter evening dresses, or 'cocktail dresses', like this one were a new concept in the 1950s. Cocktail dresses were worn for early drinks or the theatre, when daywear would not have been smart enough and a sweeping evening dress would have been too grand.

Christian Dior works on a silk coat in his Paris studio in 1952. He had a lucky break when Marcel Boussac, a leading cotton goods manufacturer and rumoured to be one of the wealthiest men in France, offered to back his first collection. At its peak, the house of Dior was reputedly grossing more than £2 million a year.

Film star Jane Russell is delighted at her fitting for an H-line creation with Dior in 1954. His H-line featured short, tight skirts which finished a couple of inches below the knee. Long jackets or slightly ballooning coats had pockets or detailing set on the hip to suggest the drop-waisted crossbar of an H.

Princess Elizabeth chats to Madame Bidault, wife of the French minister, on a visit to Versailles in 1948. She wears a modern two-piece-style ensemble, designed by Norman Hartnell. Polka dots were a popular motif for both formal daywear and informal beach dresses.

Eva Perón, better known as Evita, was the
legendary wife of Argentinian President Juan Perón.
Her sleek chignon and lavish dress with three-
quarter sleeves marks her as a high-profile client of
the house of Dior.

(Right) Fashion journalists at a Dior show in August 1955 include Marie-Louise Bousquet (with stick), Paris editor, and Carmel Snow (in white hat), editor-in-chief of *Harper's Bazaar*. For Dior's earlier collection, Snow famously coined the name New Look. Alexander Liberman, art director of American *Vogue*, is seated behind Bousquet. (Above) Photographer Richard Avedon and Diana Vreeland, Snow's successor as fashion editor of *Harper's Bazaar* and later American *Vogue*, supervise a fashion shoot for jewellery at Tiffany's. Both Avedon and Vreeland were top in their fields during the Fifties and Sixties.

Buyers attend the first show of Hubert de Givenchy in Paris, March 1952 (opposite). His prices were cheaper than the average couturier's and his style was relatively informal for couture. He created mix-and-match pieces, such as a dress with several detachable bodices that could be interchanged for different looks, as well as clothes made from men's shirting. A wide skirted, blue linen day dress shown in 1955 by Dior (right) contrasts with the slimmer suit modelled on the same catwalk.

Volume and a celebration of fabric were not limited only to skirts. This jacket is another one of Dior's, this time his fly-away line of 1948, to be teamed with a straight, tight skirt. He even designed matching boots. Dior had also extended his New Look wide skirts so that they swept the floor, for an even more extravagant look than in 1947.

Couturier Jacques Fath, who was renowned for his hourglass designs, floating panels and full skirts, here contrasts a pencil-slim skirt with a sweepingly wide, bell line coat of 1951. He sums up the two dominant silhouettes of the era in one outfit, showing wide and slim together. His later sleeveless versions of this coat had the over-collar sitting like a bolero over the rest of the coat.

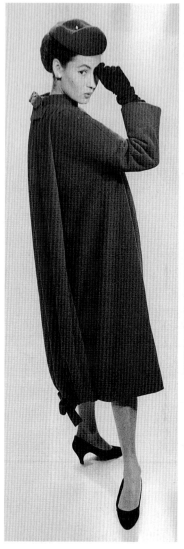

To fit over the New Look-style sweeping skirts, coats were cut wide and voluminous. Givenchy's version, 1955 (left), in brown wool keeps the volume at the back and bows suggest that the fabric has just been casually tied up rather than carefully sewn into place. Italian designer Roberto Capucci was not so subtle with his vast coat from 1956; cut to wear with a wide skirt (above), it also features detailing at the back.

This 1952 Michael of Lachasse coat, with its knife-pleated satin detailing, lets the fabric flow beautifully from the neck to achieve the wide look. Once again, the all-important back detailing is here, and the pleats which help in the construction of the garment also act as decorative detailing. Full kimono sleeves or long puffed sleeves gathered at the cuff were now back in fashion.

Various coat shapes of the Fifties are shown here. A red velvet coat by Hardy Amies (left) from 1950. The pockets sit out from the hip to emphasise the small waist. From 1954 (opposite, from the left): an A-line flared mink coat by Jean Dessès; an S-line grey flannel suit by Jacques Fath; and an H-line brown velour coat by Christian Dior.

The wide skirt and nipped-in waist were adopted for elegant summer daywear, and the halter neck from the 1930s was back in fashion. This 1953 dress by Frederick Starke emphasises the bust with its ruched neck line. Cheerful florals, spots, stripes and gingham checks were more summer favourites.

Guests at a Buckingham Palace Garden Party record the occasion with a quick snapshot at the head of the Mall, 1956. The use of the twisted seams which stretch to the hip, seen on the striped dress, were a device employed by Christian Dior to emphasise a curvaceous figure and small waist. Small, close-fitting hats, such as the one worn by the woman on the right, resembled hairpieces. They were often made of feathers, leaf-shaped leather pieces or beads threaded onto wire to make an open-mesh skullcap.

Modelled in a Parisian café, a grey-green checked dress from Norman Hartnell's 1951 low-priced ready-to-wear line, available from the department store Au Printemps (left). This is a typical day dress of the late Forties and early Fifties, with its button-front bodice and slim belt. Model Anne Gunning wears a versatile deep grey, hand-knitted dress in 1952 (opposite). With Chanel back on the scene, and 'knitting for Victory' a recent wartime hobby, knitted dresses, jumpers and cardigans were fashion favourites.

A Givenchy dress in blue piqué from 1955. London dressmakers such as Polly Peck, Frank Usher and Dorville were able to make successful ready-to-wear copies and adaptations for a fraction of the price of the couture original.

This elegant apron-cut top and tight skirt by Dior, 1955, was also copied in Britain. Some cocktail dresses at the time were held up by spaghetti straps like these. The small hat perched on top of the head is probably made from lacquered straw. Gloves had returned to their close-fitting shape after the gauntlet styles of the Thirties.

A new silhouette was launched nearly every season, driving fashion sales, with consumers wanting the new look of the season and regarding last year's as passé. (Above, left) Pierre Balmain offers the curved streamlined look in red tweed in 1953. (Above, centre) A grey tweed bat wing sleeve suit with a pouch back by Giuseppi Mattli, 1958. (Above, right) A 1949 brown herringbone suit, designed by Bianca Mosca, with a caped-back jacket which flares out at the back.

(Above, left) Dior's top-heavy suit, with an A-line-style jacket and slim skirt. It was copied by Dorville for sale on the British high street, 1955. (Above, centre) The full A-line silhouette with skirts that flare out at the hem in the shape of the letter. A Jacques Fath design, it was adapted by Polly Peck into ready-to-wear, 1955. (Above, right) A curvy S-line with slim cut, rounded back shown here as a black velour outfit, by French designer Jacques Griffe, 1954.

Italian actress Gina Lollobrigida poses in a frothy, feminine evening version of the wide-skirted dress in 1952 (left). Both Lollobrigida and Sophia Loren were known for dressing in a young, casual style, with tight trousers, printed shirts and off-the-shoulder knits. Florence was already hosting fashion shows for international buyers, and this would evolve into Milan Fashion Week. This flowing, romantic evening dress (opposite) is being modelled in Florence. Shoe designer Salvatore Ferragamo, luxury resortwear designer Emilio Pucci and eveningwear experts Roberto Capucci and Valentino were all well known at the time. Italian clothes' prices were cheaper than Paris and production was faster.

This sculptural evening gown (left) is by Cristobal Balenciaga, 1955. The off-the-shoulder cut was also used in knitwear and for blouses at the time. An equally dramatic evening dress of 1954 (opposite) is executed by Christian Dior in satin. Whereas Dior produced new looks every year and women copied his latest styles, Balenciaga evolved slowly and his pieces were more like works of art.

Rather than translating harem pants into sportswear, Jacques Fath has turned them into loose culottes in layers of pleated turquoise chiffon. The divided skirts of this 'Canasta' dress of 1952 give the effect of a skirt. The look is similar to the puffball skirts which evolved during the Eighties.

British couturier John Cavanagh gives this neat black cocktail dress of the same year a feminine touch by building it up with layers of pleated tulle. Cavanagh trained with Pierre Balmain in Paris before opening his own house in London, and, like many British designers at the time, was known for his cutting skills.

Cristobal Balenciaga plays with the notion of hidden luxury with this 1951 dress. The bodice and over-skirt are made of cotton, but the tattered petticoat-style skirt is made from silk. Balenciaga liked to contrast heavy material with feather-light fabrics such as gazar silk, a technique he demonstrates here.

Hubert de Givenchy, the Paris couturier whose mentor was Balenciaga, was known for his sculptural evening and modern, versatile daywear. This semi-fitted dress is from 1955 and here he experiments with cape-like drapery which balloons out at the back of the body. Balenciaga used a similar technique, creating dresses and cloaks that billowed away from the spine.

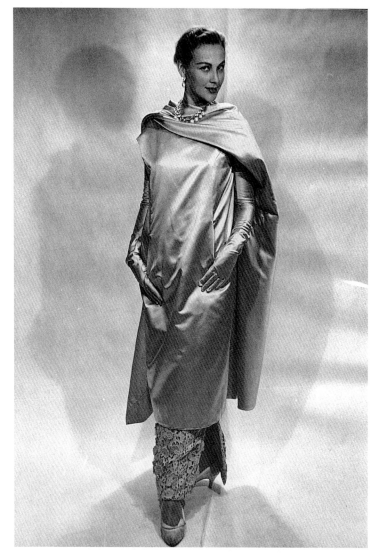

Slim-cut trousers, easy knitwear and flat, ballet-style shoes were ready-to-wear favourites in the 1950s for both women and younger girls. The look was elegant and relaxed and was worn without a hat or gloves. This is an outfit from 1955.

Housewife Ann Grierson models a black jersey top and wide skirt in 1955. Here the emphasis is on mixing and matching, and the elegant silhouette of sloping shoulders, small waist and wide skirt could be achieved by wearing separates. A wardrobe of separate skirts and tops or dresses with interchangeable bodices would offer many more possible combinations of outfits than a wardrobe of one-piece dresses and a series of suits.

The teenage and leisurewear markets produced clothes with bold prints for day, such as this two-piece summer dress by Horrocks. For evening, brocades were popular. Elsa Schiaparelli designed a cocktail dress in bright paisley cashmere lamé and Dior developed a passion for leopard skin.

An exuberant chorus girl wears a casual, swirling, printed dress as she enjoys a day at the fair in the English seaside town of Margate. In America in the Forties girls had started a trend for wide shirts, peasant-style white blouses and South American-style flounces, but the look would not have been available to British women during the war. Italian designer Emilio Pucci was best known for his swirling print designs.

Shorts were getting briefer and wider, and matching wrap-over or strapless tops were worn with them to make up 'playsuits'. This one in black cotton is designed by Frederick Starke, 1953. Jackets or beach coats were loosely cut, thigh length and often had big pockets. Raffia sun hats and flat, criss-cross sandals were fashionable beach accessories.

Mix-and-match component dressing was popular for the beach. Women wore matching bathing suits, tops and skirts which could be interchanged and layered. Here a two-piece 'playsuit' is worn underneath a split, wide skirt designed by Addie Masters. This style would be revisited in the Seventies, when hot-pants were worn under a skirt split to the waist, even at formal occasions such as weddings.

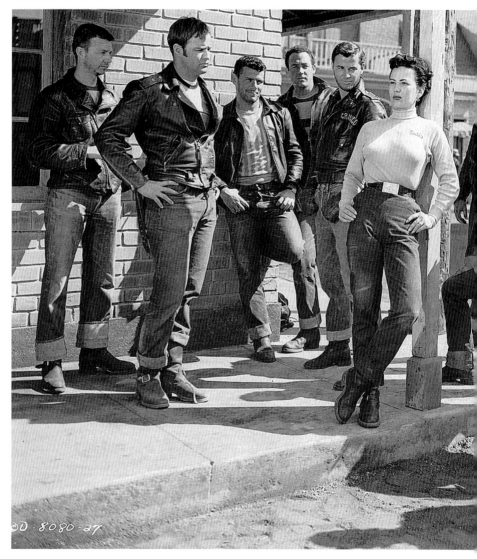

©D-8080-27

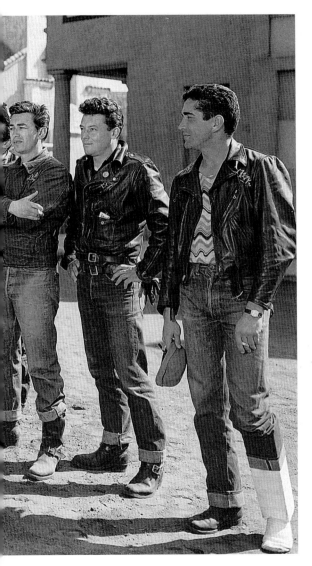

Marlon Brando (second from the left) with his biker gang, the 'Black Rebels', in a scene from the 1953 film *The Wild One*. 'Ton-up' or biker girls rode pillion on their boyfriends' motorbikes wearing unisex jeans and biker boots. Films such as *The Wild One* and *Rebel Without A Cause* influenced the look, but, rather than influencing mainstream fashion, it remained at street level. The Fifties marked the birth of teen culture. Adolescent girls no longer felt that they had to dress like their mothers: they could create their own style.

The teenage look was epitomised by the off-screen wardrobes of screen icons such as Marilyn Monroe and Brigitte Bardot, who opted to relax in casual clothes rather than maintain the perennial glamour of film stars of the Thirties. Here Monroe wears capri pants and a simple tunic-style shirt for a relaxed leisure look in 1954. She also favoured jeans and sweaters.

Twenty-two-year-old Brigitte Bardot, known as the 'Sex Kitten', runs along the beach in a photo call at Cannes in 1956. Bardot had previously been a model, and often chose simple, unshowy clothes over glamour. Her pink gingham wedding dress, designed by Jacques Esterel, brought gingham back into fashion and her wide skirts, ballet-style shoes, hooped earrings and ponytail were all widely copied.

A gaggle of giggling teenagers wear loose unisex jeans and baseball
jackets, relaxed pieces of clothing their mothers would never have
dreamt of wearing. Sales of blue jeans rocketed in the mid-Fifties. In
contrast to these girls, their more sensibly dressed peers (left) wear
wide skirts and slip-on shoes.

In America in 1956 Elvis Presley fused country music and rhythm and blues to give Fifties' youth rock 'n' roll. In Britain, fans had to make do with Tommy Steele; here they appear to be enjoying themselves at one of his concerts in 1957. These girls follow the fashionable streamlined look, wearing pencil skirts and tight jumpers which had probably been mass-produced.

Parisian students jitterbug at a night club on the Left Bank in 1949 (left) and revellers jive in New York's Greenwich Village (opposite): teen culture was in mid-swing. Girls and boys wore loose trousers, checked shirts and baseball boots. The shorter-style loose trousers were known as pedal pushers. This was the beginning of a casual, unisex daywear style that would be popular for the rest of the century.

Just as women wore culottes for cycling in the Forties, in the Fifties girls wore skirts over extra short capri pants (opposite). Italian designers such as Emilio Pucci were fast becoming known for offering a modern sportswear or leisure look. Some department stores now had areas which catered specifically for the teenage market. (Above) A young girl tries on a sweeping, printed dance dress in the Junior Miss department of a big store in 1951.

Film star Jayne Mansfield flashes her lace-trimmed bra while out on the town in Hollywood in 1951. During the Fifties the bust was emphasised by the curvaceous, slim-waisted fashions and was uplifted by pointed, underwired bras such as this one.

Weegee (Arthur Fellig) photographs a Playboy bunny girl at the beginning of the Fifties. Bunny girls, the creation of *Playboy* magazine's proprietor Hugh Hefner, were the very antithesis of the neat little housewife of the period in her floral dress and versatile, detachable apron.

Bras helped to push up the bust and mould it into a fashionable, pointed shape. Some bras were strapless and could be worn under evening dresses. Waist girdles helped to control the figure and more extreme, 8-inch, boned 'waspie' corsets were used to pull in the waist for the New Look. Some of Dior's couture dresses had figure-controlling underwear incorporated into the design. Tulle petticoats were worn to hold out wide skirts.

British film star Sabrina, formerly Norma Sykes of Blackpool, shows what a push-up-and-point bra can do for the figure. She uses a wide belt to emphasise her small waist. Tight polo necks and round necks clung to the body and showed off the figure.

Cropped trousers or capri pants and slip-on, flip-flop-style sandals were summer essentials for the fashionable woman and could be teamed with a sleeveless top or jumper. Teenagers and older women adopted this leisure look, photographed here in Rome.

French designer Maxime de la Falaise models her own designs. This pale tangerine sweater of 1954 reflects the trend for bat wing-style sleeves in tailoring of the time. She wears a matching woollen scarf around her neck. Other jumper trends included twinsets, round necks and polo necks.

The head-to-toe, fully accessorised look was something women strived for in the Fifties. (Left) Shoe shapes had become slimmer and more pointed, but open sandals with a slight platform heel were popular (right), as were shoes with a chunky high heel and an ankle strap (second from right). The bucket bag (third from right) was reputedly invented by Louis Vuitton to carry champagne. Bags in plastic, straw, fur and leather came into fashion and there was a craze for miniature, purse-style bags. British designer Edward Rayne offered upmarket court shoes (above) and bags in every colour to match an outfit. French designer Roger Vivier offered one of the first pair of stilettos, with a heel strengthened with a steel bar.

Grace Kelly wears a strapless swimming costume, 1955. It may well have been boned, with fitted support for the bust, and, like most costumes of the time, was cut low on the hips. Grace Kelly married Prince Rainier of Monaco in 1956, but died tragically in a car accident in 1982. Her name is immortalised by the Hermès Kelly bag, a square-cut design based on a saddle bag, which she was often seen carrying.

Elizabeth Taylor, here aged about eighteen, poses on the beach in a halter neck swimming costume. One-piece swimsuits rather than bikinis were still popular in America in this period. She wears full Fifties make-up: deep red lips, heavy black eye-liner and probably a pale base coloured with rouge.

Fifties skiwear now incorporated stretch ski pants made
of nylon and wool, with straps that hooked under the
foot. They were worn with brightly coloured, hooded
anoraks made out of poplin. Ski pant-shaped trousers
were also worn for daywear at the time.

Tennis player Gertrude 'Gussie' Moran shows off her bloomer-style tennis shorts worn under an open skirt, designed by Pierre Balmain for her to wear at Wimbledon in 1950. Gussie provoked even more scandal with her frilly knickers, which were most apparent when she performed a particularly fast manoeuvre on court. One of Balmain's successes was his ready-to-wear sportswear.

Hats and gloves were still needed to 'finish' a formal outfit but were no longer worn all the time. (Above, clockwise from the left) A range of popular hats. A floral hat with veil by Jean Barthot; a wide, flying saucer hat, sitting high on the forehead, by fashionable milliner Madame Paulette; a brimless, flat-topped hat in straw or felt; and a casual red felt hat in easy daywear style. (Opposite) Audrey Hepburn wears a deep hat with a turned-down brim by Givenchy in *Funny Face* (1957).

Actress Katharine Hepburn appropriated a masculine style of dressing. But, unlike Marlene Dietrich in her masculine cut suits, she wore little make-up, preferring a natural rather than a glamorous look. Here, in 1952, she wears a wide-cut trouser suit and her casual style spawned many copycats. Trousers were often worn as daywear, and designer Pucci came up with a popular design for nylon – crush-free, wide trousers known as palazzo pants.

Grace Kelly waits on the set of *To Catch A Thief* in 1955 in a sweepingly feminine evening gown. Evening dresses (rather than cocktail dresses) were usually long and often strapless with a chiffon over-skirt or floral embroidery detailing the bodice. Kelly was known for her classic style of neat suits and tapered twinsets, a marked contrast to Monroe's curvy, sex bomb image.

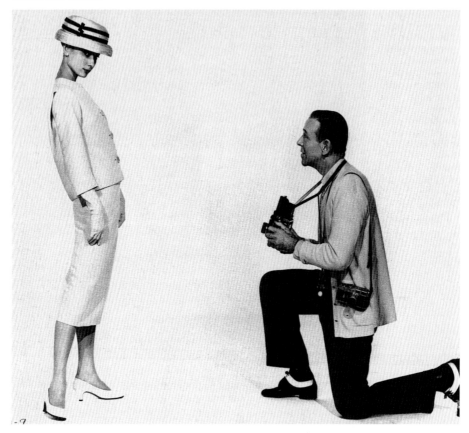

With her slim figure, Audrey Hepburn broke the accepted mould of the voluptuous film star. She was dressed on and off screen by Hubert de Givenchy, and became a walking advertisement for his clothes. Here she poses in one of his smooth suits in the 1957 film *Funny Face* (above), which also starred Fred Astaire as a fashion photographer; Hepburn's and Astaire's characters were inspired by Diana Vreeland and Richard Avedon. Hepburn adopts the all-black, street-style beatnik uniform at the end of the film (opposite).

Voluptuous curves were fashionable in the Fifties, perhaps as part of a sub-conscious return to post-war prosperity, with more food on the table and the comeback of the ultra feminine, idealised woman who no longer had to do men's work. Here Ava Gardner poses in a bodysuit in a leopard print, a pattern favoured by Christian Dior.

Sex symbol Marilyn Monroe, more than anyone else, had the curvy, womanly figure *par excellence*. Here she wears a shimmering sheath dress. American designer Norman Norell was particularly known for his sparkling sequin 'mermaid' sheath dresses as well as his fur trench coats.

Wide skirts, long veils and the use of white brocade and chiffon were back in fashion for post-war brides. For her marriage to Philip Mountbatten in 1947, Princess Elizabeth wears a dress by Royal dressmaker Norman Hartnell (above, left) which was widely copied by the mass market. She used one hundred coupons to procure her dress, as clothes rationing was not abolished until 1949. Jacqueline Lee Bouvier (above, right) favoured a lavish, skirted, off-the-shoulder dress which showed off her suntan when she married future American President John Fitzgerald Kennedy in 1953. (Opposite) Prince Rainier of Monaco marries Grace Kelly in 1956.

Audrey Hepburn's chaste white dress in white organdie by Balmain shows the sophisticated simplicity that was so much her hallmark. She married the actor Mel Ferrer in September 1954.

Brigitte Bardot's wedding to Jacques Charrier in Louveciennes, near Paris, in June 1959, was marked by its informality. Her pink gingham dress by Jacques Esterel was widely copied and helped to make gingham fashionable once again.

Waved hair which framed the face was popular during the Fifties and sleek chignons were more sophisticated. Marilyn Monroe chooses the glamorous blonde bombshell look (top, right) and Ingrid Bergman goes for feminine curls (top, left). Audrey Hepburn goes from elegant, cropped hair (above, left) to a teen-style pony tail (above, right) in the manner of Brigitte Bardot. During the Fifties hairdressers Raymond, known as 'Mr Teasie Weasie', and Antoine became celebrities.

The urchin cut – hair cut boyishly short – was adopted by some fashionable 'Bright Young Things'. Here American actress Jean Seberg shows her exaggeratedly short version in 1957, an antidote to the glossily perfect chignons and neat curls fashionable at the time.

7 Minis and Mods
1957–1966

A 1965 trapeze-style, checked wool coat by Emanuel Ungaro, showing his signature style of bold pattern and print and angular shapes. Ungaro often worked with exclusive fabrics designed by Sonja Knapp and in double thickness to ensure that the clothing held its sharp shape. This outfit is complemented by a neatly clipped hairstyle by Vidal Sassoon, the fashionable London salon.

7 Minis and Mods
1957–1966

In Paris, Yves Saint Laurent, who had trained under Dior and was expected to be his successor, alienated his Dior customers when, in 1960, he elevated beatnik and biker styles from street level to the catwalk. A year later he branched out on his own. The results were stunning: dresses influenced by the geometric style of the Dutch artist Piet Mondrian, a collection inspired by the Andy Warhol's Pop Art prints. His enduring creation was *Le Smoking*, a sleek dinner jacket for women. He combined design and retail with a chain of ready-to-wear boutiques called Saint Laurent Rive Gauche. In the late Fifties the straight up and down sack dress by Dior and Balenciaga paved the way for tunics and mini-dresses, and women rejected wide skirts for pencil skirts and nipped-in jackets. Yves Saint Laurent at Dior, Balenciaga, Pierre Balmain and Givenchy were all still forces to be reckoned with, but couture as a commercial venture was slowly dying a death.

Across the Channel, however, Mary Quant launched the mini-skirt from her King's Road boutique Bazaar, propelling fashion into a new era and setting the seal on London as the new fashion centre. The mods' neat, Italian style inspired her minimal, square-cut designs. Her child-like tunics were echoed by André Courrèges in Paris, who was also going short, but in a more robotic, Space Age style. From then on, there was no stopping the mini; hemlines just could not stop creeping up the leg. In 1983 *The Times* serialised retailer Barbara Hulanicki's book *From A to Biba*. She wrote: 'Every week I thought that we surely couldn't shorten them any more, but magically there were a few odd inches to go.'

The transition from New Look to the girl–child in her mini tunics of the late Sixties is similar to the changes between the *Belle Epoque* and the Twenties. The curvaceous, womanly corseted silhouette once more gave birth to a look of adolescent androgyny and a driving 'youth culture'. This time around the new look was epitomised by Lesley Hornby, the model better known as Twiggy.

Beatlemania, the pill, wage packets, television, the space race to the moon – everything was building up to give greater strength and power to youth culture in the mid-Sixties. The world was opening up before them. Instead of operating under ground, the new 'Bright Young Things' were about to take over and influence the mainstream. In Swinging London, ready-to-wear labels were being set up by young men and women to serve their peers, among them Thea Porter, Foale & Tuffin and Ossie Clark for Quorum. London's young designers shunned the trends from Paris and did their own thing. Boutiques sprang up everywhere: Bazaar on the King's Road, Biba on Abingdon Road, Lady Jane in Carnaby Street. New York brought the influential shop Paraphernalia and Paris snapped up Dorothée Bis. 'All classes mingled under the shop's creaking roof… Their common denominator was youth and rebellion against the Establishment. Young working girls, the beat offspring of aristocratic families, stars and would-be stars,' wrote Hulanicki.

The Sixties were a time of rebirth, of experimentation. People were excited about the Space Age and all things futuristic. Designers began experimenting with new materials. In the USA, Rudi Gernreich's research into stretch fabric led him to design topless swimming costumes for the liberated woman who wanted to let it all hang out. In Paris, Pierre Cardin experimented with plastic and came up with his own fabric, Cardine, for his stiff dresses. Mary Quant used PVC for her wet-look rainwear and there was a brief trend for disposable paper knickers.

The long, sweeping maxi-coat and the trouser suit took off, but the accepted dress for formal occasions was still a skirt, however short. In 1966 society girl Jayne Harris was barred from entering the Royal Enclosure at Ascot for wearing a white trouser suit. After a quick change in daddy's Rolls-Royce she returned wearing a buttock-skimming micro-mini-dress and was admitted.

The loud prints of Emilio Pucci, Emanuel Ungaro, the fluid Art Nouveau romanticism of the Biba style and bright colours peacock-flaunted on Carnaby Street were slowly pushing fashion out of its geometric confines. Fashion was about to turn on, tune in and drop out.

Pierre Cardin designed this voluminous scarlet draped-back coat (opposite, left) and tweed suit in 1957 (right) for his first womenswear collection. This 1958 day dress in grey alpaca by Christian Dior (opposite, right) was in the style nicknamed the 'sack'. Sack dresses were originally considered unflattering and ugly but were a transitional style that bridged the change from curvy Fifties shapes to the square-cut silhouette of the up-and-coming Sixties.

Singer Cliff Richard jives with dancer Doreen Freeman at Elstree Film Studios in Hertfordshire, just outside London, on New Year's Eve, 1958. Wide, circular rock 'n' roll skirts such as this one were worn by fashionable young women at the end of the decade, and were held out by wide nylon petticoats.

American crooner Frankie Avalon works out the new steps of the hip Californian dance 'Malibu Beat' with the cast of the film *Muscle Beach Party*, 1964. Surfing had become synonymous with American youth culture in the 1950s, and in the early Sixties the songs of groups such as the Beach Boys seemed to be entirely devoted to the sun, surf and to endless summers. Here, the bright striped clothing and bleached hair hint at the surf culture and show the rising popularity of resort-style casualwear.

In the 1960s the King's Road, Chelsea, was the haunt of the mods, a group of sartorially aware young men and women who rode Lambrettas, danced to jazz and wore neat, Italian-style clothing. Women wore short skirts or very tight hipster trousers. The fashion spread. Here, much further afield in 1963, teenage mods dance 'the Stomp' in a Sydney nightclub (opposite). Girls cropped their hair and painted their faces to look pale, and influenced Mary Quant and the resulting Sixties mainstream style. (Above) From the same year, girls dancing at the Cavern Club in Liverpool, made popular by the Beatles and other Mersey groups.

Third from the left at this 1965 audition is British actress Joanna Lumley; four years later she would receive further recognition as a Bond girl in *On Her Majesty's Secret Service*. The women's sleek mini-dresses, which still hovered near the knee, had not yet given way to very short tunic-style dresses. This picture shows some of the fashionable haircuts of the Sixties, from crop, to back-combed beehive, to long, fringed hair brushed flat.

In a celebrity line-up for a Variety Club lunch in 1965, singers Cilla Black, Petula Clark and Sandie Shaw pose for the camera in Lolita-style outfits. The bonnet-style hat, Peter Pan collars, André Courrèges-inspired Mary Jane cross-strap shoes and Empire line short dress demon-strate the Sixties trend for clothes reminiscent of childhood. The style was promoted by designer Mary Quant and sharply contrasted with the grown-up fashions of the 1950s.

Beatle John Lennon, wearing a Mary Quant (woman's) hat, waits with his wife Cynthia at London Airport in 1964. Butcher's boy sectioned hats with peaked brims like Cynthia's were worn in soft synthetics, naturals and shiny, futuristic PVC.

Leopard skin-clad actress and singer Barbra Streisand attends a Chanel catwalk show, 1966. Richard Avedon, the much-féted fashion photographer, peers over her shoulder. Buckles on bags and shoes were now popular and shoe designer Roger Vivier's pumps with tortoise-shell, mother-of-pearl or metal buckles had a major influence on mainstream fashion.

French film star Catherine Deneuve, seen here with her husband, British fashion photographer David Bailey, wears a 1966 white trapeze line coat. Double-breasted coats such as this, with two rows of buttons in a military style, were worn over a matching sleeveless shift dress or skirt for a modern take on the suit. White and silver were considered the fashionable colours of the era: they symbolised looking forward to a modern and futuristic world.

Julie Christie became a style icon during the Sixties and she won an Oscar for her role in the John Schlesinger movie *Darling* in 1965. Her loud print dress illustrates the craze for patterns of the late Sixties that was to continue into the Seventies.

Aristocratic Sixties model Veruschka von Lehndorff starred as herself in Michelangelo Antonioni's 1966 shock-factor film *Blowup* which parodied the freewheeling existence of Sixties photographers and their models. David Hemmings' character was based on photographer David Bailey and the film documented the Space Age costumes worn by the fashionable, and daring, few at the time. These models played themselves in the film and costumes were designed by Jocelyn Richards.

This curvy tweed suit of 1964 from Wallis (above, left) cost only £3 and was available in pink and navy or amber and scarlet. Also from 1964 comes a washable rose-pink 'super-mac' with glass buttons by Boussac (opposite, left). Synthetic macs, particularly in PVC, became increasingly fashionable in the Sixties. This 1964 navy crepe sheath dress (above, right) is by Pierre Cardin and is teamed with schoolgirl beret in navy felt. Berets and pillbox hats were designed to be worn perched on top of geometric hairstyles. The spring/summer 1966 white, square-cut twill coat (opposite, right) is by Giuseppe Mattli, who stopped his couture line in 1955 but kept on his ready-to-wear until the early Seventies.

This children's-style shift (opposite) in blue or pink and white checked cotton with a white pussy-cat bow in organdie is by Bernshaw and cost just over £4 at the Inexpensive Dress Department at London's Army & Navy Stores in 1963. Jean Muir's more grown-up, belted rayon jersey dress in navy (right) was more expensive, at over £18. Muir produced her first collection in 1966 and worked predominantly with fluid fabrics such as suede and jersey, achieving a look more synonymous with Seventies rather than Sixties style.

Christine Keeler arrives at court in August 1963 at the height of the Profumo affair. Keeler created more than a whiff of scandal. She was alleged to have endangered national security by sleeping with both the British Secretary of State for War, John Profumo, and a Soviet naval attaché. Her trapeze skirt and tunic top are more casual than a suit, and lace-up fastenings such as these would be made popular with Yves Saint Laurent's safari-style designs and were later taken up by the hippie movement.

Jackie Kennedy, America's First Lady, wears an outfit by French-born, American-based designer Oleg Cassini to visit the Queen in 1962. By now, Jackie was a style icon, known first for her elegant and minimalist trapeze-style suits, gilt-chained handbags, shift dresses in pale colours and, later, for her large, round 'Jackie O' sunglasses. She brought pillbox hats back into fashion (hers were by Halston) and many women copied her full hairstyle.

Yves Saint Laurent's 1965 line of dresses inspired by Dutch painter Piet Mondrian was widely copied (right) and set the tone of the Sixties with their sharp horizontal and vertical lines printed on a square-cut shift dress. Saint Laurent set up Rive Gauche, his ready-to-wear boutiques, in 1966, and (opposite, right) the actress Catherine Deneuve poses in his Paris boutique in one of his modern black dresses. For the summer of 1965 Deneuve wears Space Age white (opposite, left); her flat, equally Space Age white boots in PVC or leather, made fashionable by André Courrèges, were often teamed with mini-skirts.

A more formal suit in heavy white linen from the Boutique Collection by Yves Saint Laurent, 1964 (left), contrasts with his informal mini-skirt, thick tights and striped jumper of 1966 (opposite). Saint Laurent himself seen outside is his newly opened Rive Gauche boutique. Stretch tops, knits and all-in-one jumpsuits were often hooded, a style which hinted at space helmets and a unisex style.

(Above) In a scene from the classic 1960 film *La Dolce Vita*, Anita Ekberg makes an arrival. (Opposite, clockwise, from top left) Elizabeth Taylor strolls in Rome's Piazza Navona in 1962, sporting a Fifties resort-style look; Princess Grace of Monaco (formerly the actress Grace Kelly), accompanied by her husband, carries an eponymous Kelly bag by Hermès. Motown group the Supremes arrive at Heathrow Airport in 1965 with glamorous furs to ward off the chill of an English spring day; Gina Lollobrigida chooses a feminine day dress in 1960. Leopard skin was a hallmark of Christian Dior, and spike heels and pointed shoes were still in fashion in the early Sixties.

Actress Linda Christian takes coffee on a summer's evening in Capri in 1958. Her printed puffball-style skirt, with its hem pulled under and up rather than sliced off, is a style that was to come back into fashion during the 1980s. Yves Saint Laurent created a puffball, 'Barbaresque' evening dress for Dior. At the end of the Fifties, designers were experimenting with volume, with billowing backs on coats, loose bat wing sleeves on dresses and puffed-up bodices.

April in Paris. Jackie Kennedy smiles for the camera at a ball at the end of the Fifties. Popular evening dresses of the time were strapless and caught under the bust, in the Empire line style, either with a small, flat bow or a more exaggerated, billowing bow. The dresses were fitted and wide-skirted at the back, but a great tuck of fabric was caught up at the front, as if by the bow, and it flowed straight down from there to the floor, with no suggestion of a waist.

Italian designer Valentino Garavani opened a couture house in Rome in 1959 and quickly became known for his elegant, feminine and flattering clothes: his label survives into the 21st century. Valentino's fluid, opulent, Eastern-style over-tunic and pleated chiffon pyjama pants of 1966 (left) give an evening twist to wide palazzo pants. British designer John Cavanagh's printed silk evening pyjamas from 1965 (opposite, left) work with an over-layer of chiffon rather than with an under-layer. A double jersey, black Empire line dress of 1963 is, in contrast, svelte and elegant (opposite, right).

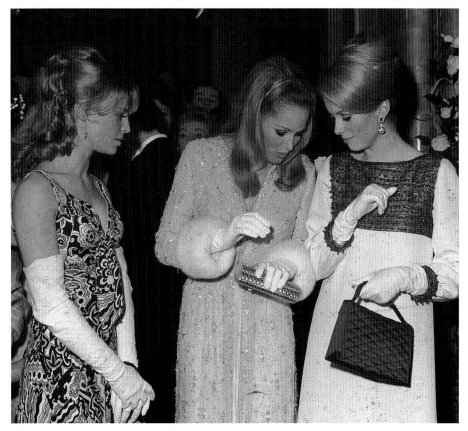

A galaxy of film stars. (Above) Julie Christie, Ursula Andress and Catherine Deneuve look glamorous at the 1966 Royal Film Performance. Quilted bags were a Chanel hallmark and Empire line dresses and white fur trims were popular for bridalwear as well as for the evening. (Opposite, clockwise, from top left) Audrey Hepburn wears a white satin evening dress in 1961; Elsa Martinelli, accompanied by Kenneth More, shows off the fashionable boat-shaped neck line in 1957; Gina Lollobrigida wears a frilled summer dress made popular by Christian Dior and a fashionable pillbox hat, 1965; Claudia Cardinale poses in an evening cape and dress in 1962.

Cathy McGowan, fashionable presenter of Sixties television pop music programme *Ready Steady Go*, models one of her own clean-cut tunic dresses in 1965. The programme also provided a forum from which to show off the latest fashions. Aware that designers waited with bated breath every week in the hope that she would wear one of their outfits, Cathy McGowan took advantage of the publicity generated by designing her own line.

Mary Quant accepts the Society of Industrial Artists and Designers Medal for 1966, the same year that she set up her own branded line of cosmetics. Quant trained at Goldsmiths College of Art in London and went on to open Bazaar, her shop in the King's Road. She graduated from selling clothing to making up her own simple, child-like, brightly coloured tunics, as seen here, and soon became one of the stars of 1960s 'Swinging London'.

Designers also magnified the intricate black and white Op Art patterns, so that sometimes all that remained were large panels of black and white decorating dresses or coats. The simple shape of a wool jersey dress by Naka of Milan at the Italian Knitwear Show in 1966 (left) is emphasised by the black and white lines. Black and White come together as singer Cilla Black (real name Priscilla White) models a geometrically patterned day dress (opposite).

American manufacturer Larry Aldrich commissioned Op Art-style fabrics, heavily influenced by artist Bridget Riley, from textile designer Julian Tomchin to make up into clothing. Sixties designers such as Ossie Clark and Pierre Cardin included the black and white geometric motifs in their collections. This evening dress for autumn/winter 1965 is by Roberto Capucci. The semi-psychedelic motifs were revived for the second 'Summer of Love' and the Acid House movement in 1988.

This 1966 Italian couture dress in the Op Art style is also by Roberto Capucci. The wide sleeves of the dress were very much a mid-Sixties trend for eveningwear and bridalwear. Trouser suits and long dresses, as well as mini-dresses, were still popular evening-wear styles.

A fake oilcloth coat is promoted here as eveningwear for the Christmas party season of 1962. Synthetic PVC, dracon and vinyl clothing was more commonly worn for daywear, and hip-length PVC 'scooter jackets' were particularly popular. Such materials had never before been considered suitable for casual clothing, and some clothing, or 'body-armour', was even made of moulded synthetic materials which set hard when finished.

Mary Quant set a trend for PVC clothing when she developed wet-look rainwear. This black wet-weather oilskin outfit of 1963, which includes matching accessories, still sports children's-style Peter Pan collars. Quant adopted a cartoon-style daisy for her logo; it would become a hallmark of the age and influenced the coming Flower Power revolution.

In the Sixties new, sometimes tiny, boutiques sprang up offering the latest fashions, more often than not run by young people who understood the Sixties scene, its fashions and the demands of their clientele. Carnaby Street, initially known for its menswear boutiques, and the King's Road became the stamping ground of fashionable Swinging London. The Beatles opened Apple. Model Paulene Stone (right) wears a velvet coat from Apple in 1967.

Shops like Biba and Bus Stop were big hits in London, as was Irving Sellars' boutique Mates in Carnaby Street, which catered for both men and women.

French summer resortwear from 1958 by Boussac is modelled on a London street (above), showing how the wide coats and dress shapes of formalwear couture could be translated into informal beach clothes and combined with shorts and capri pants. (Opposite) Model Maggie Auld wears a daringly sheer, white lace dress over a white bikini from Christian Dior's 1966 spring collection. The same year saw a trend for short, revealing micro-dresses in white lace with flared cuffs set on three-quarter length sleeves.

Bikini-clad holiday-makers outside the Carlton Hotel in Cannes in 1958 enjoy a glass of wine (opposite), and Bianca Volpato soaks up the rays in a lilac bikini on Capri in the same year (right). In the late Fifties and early Sixties bikinis were worn slung low on the hip, and had detachable halter neck straps or strings which tied at the back of the neck. Flip-flops, straw bags and straw hats or headscarves completed the essential beach look.

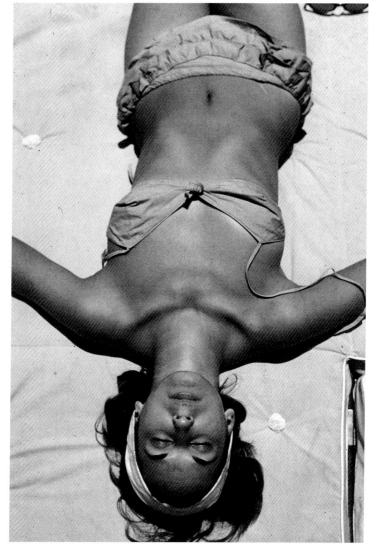

Eternal French pop stars Johnny Hallyday and Sylvie Vartan escape from the
church by a side door after their wedding in April 1965 in order to avoid the
press. Separate hoods or scarves worn with wedding dresses were alternatives
to veils at the time, and more radical bridalwear included fur-trimmed mini-
dresses worn with white boots and a fur-trimmed bonnet.

Fashion model Carol Chilvers marries fashion photographer Frank Sweeney in June 1966. Her maxi-coat or dress worn over trousers, with a pillbox hat rather than a veil, was an unconventional approach. The bride's sister Marilyn even wears Bermuda shorts rather than a skirt or dress, her bonnet adding the final, fashionable touch.

Hats for women. (Left, left to right from the top) A man's cloth trilby by Pierre Cardin for women in 1962; a cheeky butcher's boy cap from 1963; Baroness Thyssen, the former fashion model Fiona Campbell-Walker, chooses a fashionable down-turned brim hat from 1963. Headscarves, hoods and bonnets were also popular: Elizabeth Taylor wraps her head up in 1962. In 1966 Space Age felt helmet hats were offered by Pierre Cardin, and in 1962 Claudia Cardinale chooses a rain hat style in felt with a softened, waved brim.

By the mid-Sixties, hats were expected to be worn only for formal occasions such as weddings and at the races; they were therefore used to make a fashion statement. During the Sixties hats generally had short, down-turned brims and an elongated crown like a beehive hairstyle; berets, caps, rain hats and headscarves could be popped neatly over fashionably short hair. This mock-croc hat of 1963 is by Chez Elle and was available from Harvey Nichols Little Shop.

Hairdresser Vidal Sassoon's asymmetric pudding basin style was, in every sense, at the cutting edge of hair fashion, and was initially worn by Mary Quant. Sassoon also developed the 1963 'Nancy Kwan' cut, a bob that was cut short at the nape of the neck. This picture shows the fashionable whitened face, pale lips and exaggerated, over-made-up eyes with false eyelashes that were important make-up trends. Boyishly cropped hair was now as fashionable as it had been in the Twenties. Twiggy took up the look, but some women just covered up their long hair with short wigs.

Jean Shrimpton shows off her 'sun' hairstyle, designed by Parisian hair stylist Carita, in 1965. The 'Shrimp's' long, straight tresses were much imitated, and women also built their hair high up on their heads, using back-combing or hairpieces pinned with bows for a late Fifties and early Sixties look. The high styles were then set and sprayed to ensure that they would not collapse.

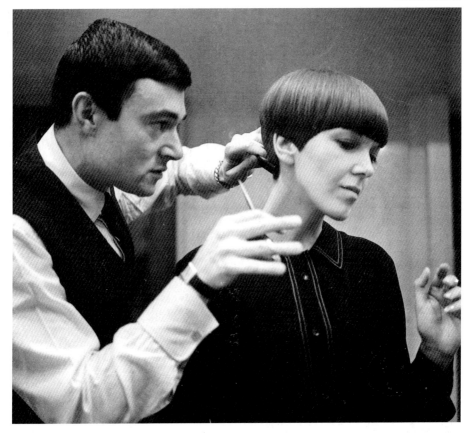

(Above) Mary Quant has her hair cut in 1964 by Vidal Sassoon, the most fashionable hairdresser of the Sixties, in the famous five-point cut which she made her own. Others had their favourite styles. (Opposite, left to right from the top) In 1966 Jean Shrimpton keeps her hair long; Elizabeth Taylor goes for a more full-bodied style in 1960; Twiggy looks child-like in a crop. Veronica 'Ronnie' Bennett from the Ronettes has a beehive style in 1964; singer Alma Cogan goes for the full-bodied, short style in 1962; actress Tippi Hedren piles her hair high up on her head in 1963; singer Dusty Springfield holds onto her back-combed hair in 1964; and Diana Ross, lead singer with the Supremes, goes for big hair in 1965.

8 The Daisy Age

1967–1978

'Make Love Not War' became the mantra of the flower children of the Sixties and Seventies. The 'Love' sunglasses and CND logo dress of 1967 were for those who felt the need to make a sartorial, anti-aggression statement. The clean cut of the dress and the model's cropped hair are more early Sixties mod style than flower child. 1967 may have been known as the 'Summer of Love', but a month before this picture was taken an anti-war demonstration outside the Pentagon, Washington, DC, had escalated into violence, resulting in some two hundred and fifty arrests.

8 The Daisy Age
1967–1978

Free your mind and your clothes will follow. The Summer of Love, Jimi Hendrix, Vietnam protests, bra-burning and LSD. Flower power and psychedelia swept up the baby boomers in a stream of pot smoke. Man was about to walk on the moon and anything, it seemed, could happen. Fashion rejected geometric futurism for a longer length, romantic style. Retailer and designer Carole Austen was quoted in *International Textiles* in 1970: 'As far we can see we will have a mixture of casualness, fluidity and fantasy.'

The world was shrinking fast as air travel became more affordable. Western society became more aware of its place in a multicultural environment. Designers played with global references, Kenzo with his native Japan and Yves Saint Laurent with Africa and China. Souvenirs from the hippie trails soon worked themselves into women's wardrobes: shaggy Afghan coats, Indian cheesecloth shirts, South American ponchos and patchwork gypsy skirts.

Womenswear was flamboyant and menswear was not far behind. Zandra Rhodes and Ossie Clark dressed women in yards of printed chiffon so that they resembled psychedelic butterflies. Pop stars set the trends. David Bowie was performing in full glam rock outfits and boys were now allowed to strut their stuff. A 1967 extract from *The Ossie Clark Diaries* (1998) reads: 'Brian Jones and Keith [Richards] took to wearing the silks and satins printed by Celia and the skin-tight jewel coloured trousers from a stash of pre-war corset satin AP found. I made men's shirts with frills in chiffon, in crepe, with a one-sided collar, a leather jacket metallic with blue snake. Marianne [Faithfull] bought a suede suit trimmed in python with a fluted peplum and never asked the price.' Unisex flared jeans and T-shirt became a street uniform, men and women grew their hair and girls now wanted trousers rather than skirts.

The individual was free to choose from a myriad styles. The new trends kept on coming: minis, maxis and midis; harem pants, hot pants and velvet knickerbockers. Second-hand no longer meant second-best. In London, boutiques such as Granny Takes A Trip encouraged the modern woman to raid the past and create her own look. The British high street also offered cheap alternatives to designer clothes, Laura Ashley with its crisp cotton peasant style and Biba, which had by now moved to a large store in Kensington, with bohemian romance in crushed velvet.

When punk gobbed its way down the streets of London and New York it traded on the shock factor for attention. Women wore tight leathers, leopard skin, and bondage trousers and either stomped around in their Doc Marten boots or strutted in stilettos. Bodies were pierced, hair was shaved, dyed and spiked and everything was customised with chains, paint and safety pins. Punk still stands out as one of the best granny-shocking movements of the century. Vivienne Westwood and Malcolm McLaren were the puppeteers of punk, selling the clothes from their King's Road shop Seditionaries and launching the Sex Pistols, who provided the soundtrack for the movement. Inevitably, punk hit the catwalk: in 1977 Zandra Rhodes did designer safety pins.

In the late Seventies designers moved from the theatrical to the practical. A new wave of ready-to-wear designers began to offer an antidote to fussy, over-the-top designs. Jean Muir designed minimal jersey pieces in London; Sonia Rykiel sold stylish knitwear in Paris; and in Italy Giorgio Armani offered basics for the working woman. In America, Calvin Klein and Ralph Lauren launched designer jeans and Halston did sleek jersey trouser suits and dresses. Milan had now established itself as the fashion capital of Italy, with its signature luxury sports style, fine furs at Fendi and elegance at Valentino. Designers such as these were offering women versatile, modern wardrobes. Fashion would shed its psychedelic skin and move on to the Eighties, taking with it these basic, modern concepts.

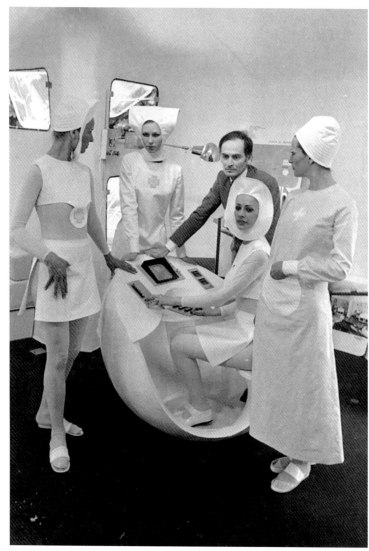

Modern uniforms live up to the Sixties reputation. Pierre Cardin presents his new designs for nurses' uniforms in the hospital unit at Boulogne in 1970 (left). Even harder to believe are these mini-dressed hostesses working on British Rail's Advanced Passenger Train in 1972 (opposite). Have they perhaps forgotten to put on their trousers?

(Above, left) Designer Paco Rabanne shows a metal disc mini-dress, 1968. He also experimented with plastic, metal and leather for his chain-mail creations. Rabanne started his career selling extravagant jewellery and plastic buttons to Paris couturiers. (Above, right) French singer Françoise Hardy apparently laboured for over an hour to put on this all-in-one outfit of linked metal pieces in 1968. Boilersuits for marching women were not the only all-in-one option: streamlined jumpsuits and catsuits were made in more luxurious fabrics and could look both sexy and glamorous.

(Above, left) Pierre Cardin uses clean, easy lines to create a modern Space Age suit in powder grey. Cardin had moved on from the short mini-dresses of the Sixties and taken up the new long silhouette of the Seventies for his 1972 collection. Skullcaps from the Thirties were revitalised, and cut-out panels, such as the one on the pocket, were a Cardin trademark. White and silver were the modern, futuristic colours of the 1960s. Here (above, right) Moscovite Galina Milovskaya models Russian-designed silver leggings and a red fox fur jacket in 1968.

A leather chain-mail coat designed by Paco Rabanne, 1967 (opposite). The dress (right), in a children's style from the late Sixties, is by André Courrèges and is combined with mary jane shoes, which were originally designed for children before being adopted as an adult style. The calf-length socks created the same silhouette as fashionable white boots, for which Courrèges is renowned.

Shorter and shorter skirts were now being worn every day (above), and the dress on the right follows the baby doll nightwear style. This picture shows British actress Maureen Lipman (left) and fellow members from the cast of the 1967 film *Up The Junction*. (Opposite) Sixties super-model Twiggy shows how a classic shirt dress from her own collection, with its raised skirt and long collars, can be made to look modern in 1967.

Pierre Cardin waits with his models at his autumn/winter fashion show of 1971.
Cardin was renowned for his dramatic but clean designs. During the 1960s he
designed tight leather trousers and bat wing trousers, and tabard tops to be worn
over trousers. As well as haute couture, Cardin produced ready-to-wear collections
which he sold through his boutiques, first Eve and then Adam.

Even though Cardin's face is hidden behind a bizarre aluminium mask, Elizabeth Taylor seems happy enough to try and strike up a conversation. Her elaborate headdress is made up of orchids and lilies punctuated with silver spikes. Before opening his couture house in 1957, Cardin had run a business providing costumes for fancy dress balls and the theatre.

André Courrèges designed this blue 'cosma' jacket (left) studded with silver spangles for 1974, a softer style altogether than his earlier stark, Space Age looks. He took his influence from the male wardrobe, and the slouchy comfort of this outfit has the easiness of a man's jacket and trousers. For 1973, Paco Rabanne has also changed tack: this body armour coat (opposite) is in macramé-look leather links for a 'crafty', natural look more in line with the Seventies ethos.

Barbara Hulanicki (opposite) was the inspiration behind Biba, the influential boutique which offered women cheap clothes in a romantic, Art Nouveau style, including wide-brimmed hats and long, fluid trousers. Starting as three small shops, in 1973 Biba expanded into a department store in Kensington High Street but its success was short-lived; by 1975 financial problems had forced Hulanicki to shut up shop. (Above) Bargain-hunters sort through feathers during the closing down sale.

Jackie Onassis (née Kennedy) leaves an Athens nightclub at seven in the morning with her husband Aristotle Onassis, after celebrating her fortieth birthday party. Empire line dresses were often worn for the evening. Jackie's short version from 1969 is decorated with the bright psychedelic patterns so popular at the time.

Models for the Clothing Export Council in summer 1969 express their passion for Richard Nixon in his bid for the American presidency. Although Dick was popular at the time, in 1974 he became the first President to resign, under threat of impeachment. The double-breasted, high-waisted coat worn by the woman on the left became a wardrobe essential for women in the late Sixties and Seventies, and was worn with square-toed shoes or knee-length boots.

Brigitte Bardot (opposite) takes a break from her busy filming schedule in London in 1966, while Claudia Cardinale (right) poses for the cameras in Salzburg in 1968. Mini-skirts, boots and polo necks were a casual uniform for daywear and Italian design label Missoni was well known for its striped, knitted outfits. High-heeled ankle boots and cowboy boots were also popular as an alternative to longer boots.

This 1972 velvet coat, in a nostalgic, children's style, is worn with long, striped, ribbed stockings. Sheer stockings were now less fashionable, and, when tights were not worn, stockings were often ribbed and thick or striped, with bold geometric motifs.

This 1970 student-style outfit from Paris demonstrates the trend for stripes, crochet tights and long student scarves. In typically Parisian style, the look still manages to be elegant, especially when compared with the earthy hippie looks coming out of London and San Francisco at the same time. Paris-based knitwear designer Sonia Rykiel designed relaxed, elegant knitwear separates and experimented with striped motifs, as did the boutique and label Dorothée Bis.

Mini-skirts moved further and further up the thigh, and the one on the left, from 1968, is little more than a tunic. This photograph shows young entrepreneurs Sarah Buadpiece and Debbie Torrens outside their boutique, To Jump Like Alice. Boutique mania spread during the Sixties, with young people opening shops to provide fashionable clothing for their peers.

In 1967, window shoppers in the King's Road show how to wear a printed tunic: with or without trousers. Thigh-high boots would be worn with Robin Hood-style tunic dresses four years later, but here knee boots make what almost amounts to a gesture of modesty when they are teamed with such a short skirt.

Before hemlines took the plunge with the maxi-skirt, mini-skirts were getting shorter all the time. These racegoers (left) brave Ascot in 1968 wearing very short dresses; a year later (above) skirts had crept even higher. 1969 was known as the 'year of the micro-mini'.

American actress Raquel Welch strides through Rome's Spanish Square (above, left). Skinny-rib polo necks and high necks were worn by both men and women with jeans or under a suit for a more formal look. Actress Charlotte Rampling is seen here (above, right) in a high-collared, Edwardian-style shirt. On the high street, shops like Laura Ashley and Mr Freedom offered women pretty clothes, some of them reminiscent of Edwardian and Victorian underwear, and simple summer dresses in cotton and corduroy.

Jeanne Lanvin's romantic summer 1968 wedding dress (right) reflects the idealised, pastoral look so much in demand at the time. (Opposite, clockwise, from top left) Show business dresses up (and down) for its weddings. Actress Sharon Tate marries film director Roman Polanski in January 1968 in a daringly short mini-dress; pop singer Lulu emerges from the church with new husband Maurice Gibb of the Bee Gees in 1969. Fur trims and bonnets and scarves were an alternative to a veil. In the same year singer Cilla Black rejects traditional white for a dark velvet mini-dress for her wedding to Bobby Willis, her personal manager. Bianca marries Mick Jagger in a white trouser suit in St Tropez in 1971.

Exaggerated felt hats such as this were often worn with scarves and gold link chains tied around the high crown. The picture from 1967 demonstrates the fashionable Sixties make-up of the time: pale lips and face, heavy black liquid eyeliner and fake eyelashes.

Mini, maxi or midi? That was the question in 1969 as all three were fashionable. Pierre Cardin offered a solution – a long maxi-coat (which could almost be a dress) that flipped open to reveal a mini-skirt; hot-pants could be worn in the same way. In a similar vein, designers slashed long skirts in strips to the thigh so that the panels flared out to reveal the leg.

Fashion model Hazel, posing in a London street, shows off a crepe playsuit with a divided skirt, designed by Ossie Clark for the summer of 1973. Her platform shoes make her legs look even longer than they really are.

The multitalented Mary Quant also put her name on underwear, stockings and footwear and had started her wholesale manufacturing operation, Ginger Group, in 1963. These shoes and boots are from her autumn 1971 collection. From left to right: 'Pin Up', a wedge shoe in grey and cream; 'Plantagenet', a boot in blue suede with ribbon detailing; 'Sprinter', a wedge heel, tie-front shoe; and 'Jacob's Ladder', a suede boot with lace-up detailing at the back.

A maxi-coat as worn on a London street in 1969. Maxis were still worn with mini-skirts but they would soon be paired with long, flared trousers. Military buckles worn as fastenings make references to army greatcoats. The pom-pommed, fur-trimmed bonnet marks the final flourish of children's-style dresses during the Sixties, and similar hats also appeared as bridalwear.

By 1969, Pierre Cardin's designs had moved on to embrace the new longer length skirts, but his style, as shown here, is still clean and minimal. Throughout the next decade Cardin continued to play a major part in fashion. Accessories such as the metal buckles on the models' belts were sometimes incorporated into mini-dresses during the Sixties for a *Star Trek* look.

As trousers and cuffs flared, so did coats, wraps and kaftans. This elegant red wool coat by Pierre Balmain was made for his autumn/winter 1974 collection, and his capes and wraps in the Cossack style were much copied.

Capes and kaftans offered a fluid alternative to more structured coats, could be worn for day or evening, and would sit over a long, flared skirt or a pair of trousers. For autumn/winter 1971, this wool cape is executed in deep maroon.

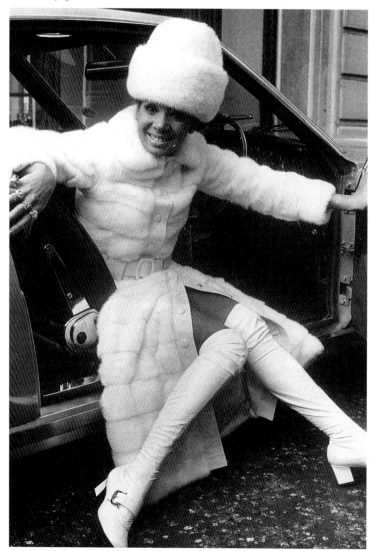

A ring on every finger, singer Shirley Bassey emerges from her Aston Martin clad in white mink in 1970. Never one to play down her appearance, her style always exuded affluence. Fur worn in bands on coats like this was also popular at the time for short bomber jackets or knee-length coats.

This more classic printed coat of 1969 (above, left) was typically worn with a skirt or dress of the same length underneath, and this student-style coat of 1970 (right) is a shorter version of the maxi-coat. Combined with a knitted scarf and hat, it offers a less extreme, more down-to-earth style than the hippie look, and is reminiscent of outerwear worn by Victorian children.

American pop star Marsha Hunt performing at the Isle of
Wight Pop Festival in September 1969, where Bob Dylan
was also playing. Afro haircuts like Hunt's became popular
with both men and women at the time.

Elizabeth Taylor struts her stuff in a hot-pants suit, 1971. During the height of the trend, hot-pants were acceptable for the office and were even worn at weddings, under a skirt split to the waist.

In 1976, American actress Jodie Foster played a twelve-year-old prostitute in *Taxi Driver*. She wore large, round 'Jackie O' glasses and a wide-brimmed, floppy hat, the fashionable, romantic accessories of the time.

Jeans could be customised in many ways. This woman (left) has cut hers down to hot-pants and customised them with studs for the summer in St Tropez in 1972. Studded bracelets and belts were also fashionable, pre-empting the punk trend that would come later. Hot-pants, however, were not always flattering; these tourists (opposite) climbing the steps to St Paul's Cathedral in 1971 might have been tempted to cover up.

Model Michelle Tucker turns mechanic for the camera in 1971. Her velvet hot-pants have acquired a dungaree-style bib; others had straps resembling braces. Hot-pants, which came into fashion in 1970, were the short alternative to the long skirts in fashion at the time.

Stewardesses working for Southwest Airlines of Texas in 1972 had to look good in hot-pants and kinky boots to get the job in the first place. In flight, they served drinks with names like Passion Punch and Love Potion. Long boots and coloured tights were often worn with hot-pants, just as they were with mini-skirts, and boots at the time sported thick, square high heels and sometimes platform soles.

Jean Shrimpton signs a book of protest against British complicity in the Nigerian–Biafran War on Christmas Eve, 1969. The sometime girlfriend of photographer David Bailey, Jean Shrimpton became, with Twiggy, one of the faces of the Sixties. Here her small frame and long legs are engulfed in one of the shaggy 'yeti' coats that were particularly fashionable at the time.

1971 Women's Lib protesters parade the housewife's shopping bag and apron-form crucifix during a 4,000-strong march to No. 10 Downing Street. The real hard-line protester's uniform of choice was the boilersuit, but these women obviously prefer furs, jeans and double-breasted coats with large collars typical of the Seventies.

Women marched for their rights in 1971. Afghan sheepskin coats, the leather traditionally cured in urine, were originally picked up on the Eastern hippie trail. Scarves tied around the head, gypsy-style, would be combined with long, patchwork skirts. Hand-knitting and crochet, such as these snake-like scarves and knitted berets, were the reaction against the wipe-clean PVC and smooth lines of the 1960s.

Actress Jane Fonda drums up support at an anti-Vietnam War rally in Washington, DC, in 1970. She would later star in, and win an Oscar for, *Coming Home*, a film about war veterans returning from Vietnam. Long tie-dye and psychedelic printed scarves were looped around the neck, worn as headbands or just thrown over one shoulder. She wears a T-shirt, which had been adopted as womenswear in the 1960s, but no bra. Has she burnt it, in true Seventies style?

Feminist lawyer and politician Bella Abzug demands liberation for women on a New York street in 1970. Capes, such as the paisley one she is seen wearing in the photograph, were once again back in fashion alongside more casual-style ponchos. Both offered a more relaxed alternative to coats.

Actress Edina Ronay (left), later to become a notable knitwear designer, struts her stuff at a 1968 film premiere. Felt hats like the one she is wearing were also worn with high, more exaggerated crowns, or with wider floppy brims using flowers and scarves as trims. Blues/rock singer Janis Joplin (opposite) goes for the full global, androgynous hippie look in the same year with her Afghan coat, long hair and tasselled top.

For once Julie Christie eschews glamour with her earth mother-style crochet blanket and bedraggled hair. Her bag is large and chunky as befits the times; other styles included patchwork leather, the most luxurious in lizard skin, large carpet-bags and handbags decorated with wooden beads. David Lean's *Dr Zhivago* (1965), in which Julie Christie played Lara, helped inspire the trend for rough-look sheepskin jackets and maxi-coats.

Teenage pupils from Holland Park School in London get the 1971 look with Afghan coats, wide-sleeved tunic shirts, basket-weave bags and jeans. Blue jeans had never been more popular. They were often worn with bell-bottoms, as seen here, and combined with a T-shirt for casual dressing. Popular brands included Lee, Wrangler and Levi. The Seventies also marked the birth of designer jeans. Gloria Vanderbilt's tight, buttock-hugging white jeans were particularly coveted.

Twenty-three-year-old Ann Rochon from Paris, in full hippie regalia, waits for a train at London's Waterloo Station, on her way to the 1970 Isle of Wight Pop Festival. Her crushed velvet trousers and matching waistcoat were worn by both men and women at the time. Long beads and Indian jewellery, including belly and ankle chains, were popular, as were opulent Eastern scarves like the one she wears here. Bag-belts were introduced by Sonia Rykiel and pocket purses were designed to button on and off items of clothing.

A flower child sits it out at the Legalise Pot Rally in London's Hyde Park in 1967. Flowers became one of the dominant motifs associated with the era, particularly the daisies on this girl's dress. Flower mania stemmed from the cartoon flower motif adopted by designer Mary Quant as her logo, and psychedelic floral prints soon appeared on skirts, dresses and shirts.

T-shirts were worn closely fitted to the body (right), and 1920s skullcaps and headbands came back into fashion again as women adopted flowing, layered robes. These two girls are at the 1969 Stones in the Park concert, where Mick Jagger, wearing an androgynous white, frilled shirt-dress, released thousands of butterflies in memory of the late Brian Jones. (Opposite) Hair was parted in the middle and worn long by men and women and jeans were customised with paint, appliqué and patchwork.

Peace, love, and the hippie trail flung Indian yogis and meditating in ashrams into fashion. Thin cheesecloth tunic shirts, long, embroidered skirts and strings of bead were just some of the fashions brought back and adopted from India. This seminal photograph (left) taken at Rishekesh in India in 1968 includes (from left to right) Pattie Boyd, John Lennon, Mike Love of the Beach Boys, the Maharishi Mahesh Yogi, George Harrison, Mia Farrow, unidentified person, Donovan, Paul McCartney, Jane Asher and Cynthia Lennon. (Above) Actress Anita Pallenberg wears a loose Eastern kaftan.

This 1969 outfit by Angela Gore typified the nostalgic English country look targeted at townees. Laura Ashley, who started out selling printed scarves and kitchen cloths, was best known for her country look. She produced long, pretty dresses in flower prints and pinafore dresses that could be worn over high-necked shirts. A wide floppy hat would complete the look.

The whirling skirts of this 1970 Miss Selfridge maxi-dress are in complete contrast to the geometric minis of the 1960s. It was available in black, purple and brown and cost £11. This style of dressing was known as the 'Granny look'. Shawls and lace-up boots finished the look. Wide cut kaftans and ponchos offered a different version of the long flowing style, giving more of a global twist.

Designers borrowed references from around the globe and produced opulent, Eastern-style embellished and embroidered eveningwear laced with gold. Yves Saint Laurent's Russian collection is particularly remembered for this. These fluid sequinned and embroidered gowns (left) are from 1974. The house of Lanvin produced this 1968 evening dress (opposite, left), with a Sixties-style Empire line cut, and couturier Ted Lapidus designed a more fluid version of this look (opposite, right) later in 1975.

Pop stars and their girlfriends took to wearing matching or unisex outfits. (Above) John Lennon and Yoko Ono wear white suits in 1969. (Opposite, clockwise, from top left) Rolling Stones guitarist Keith Richards wears a three-piece suit, while girlfriend Anita Pallenberg looks as if she has borrowed his hat, 1971; Mick Jagger and Bianca both wear skirts in St Tropez in 1971; three years earlier, Marianne Faithfull and Jagger sport velvet over white shirts; in 1969 Rolling Stone Brian Jones and friend both choose belted, mid-tone coats.

A young Marie Helvin poses in a cotton kimono by Tokyo couturier Kansai Yamamoto in 1971, the year he opened his design house. Yamamoto crossed traditional Japanese dress with Western clothing. Together with Hanae Mori, Yuki, Yohji Yamamoto and Issey Miyake, he introduced Japanese design to an international audience in the 1970s.

Emanuel Ungaro is flanked by models wearing pieces from his spring/summer 1971 collection. During the Sixties his sharp, angular designs set him apart from other designers because he favoured bold prints and patterns, themes he has continued ever since. Here Ungaro uses the popular flower power daisy motif and gypsy-style scarves. Dashingly tall hats, like the one on the right, were very popular during the Seventies.

This fluid trouser suit of 1968 by Ossie Clark and Alice Pollock is accessorised with a matching gypsy-style headscarf. Celia Birtwell, who married Clark, designed most of his prints; often bold but romantic, they had names such as 'Floating Daisy' and 'Lapis Lazuli'.

The androgynous, dashing cavalier look swung into fashion in 1970, and both girls and boys could now wear satin trousers and frilled shirts. Yves Saint Laurent had introduced velvet knickerbockers and trousers tucked into long boots such as these (right) to be worn in the 'Cossack' style, teamed with wide fur hats and sashes tied at the waist. The peacock print of the frilled shirt is by Sheila Hudson for Thea Porter.

This swirling Art Deco print dress of 1971 is by Jeff Banks, who was later to become involved with the highly successful multiple retailer Warehouse Utility. Banks was known for providing fashionable, affordable clothing for women during the Seventies. The shirt and matching handkerchief point skirt cost £15 for the pair.

Bold prints, part-
icularly those with
psychedelic colours
and patterns,
became desirable.
Ossie Clark (with
prints by Celia
Birtwell) and Zandra
Rhodes were known
for their printed
designs. This tribal
pattern was
designed by Liberty,
and made up into a
button-through shirt-
dress and matching
scarf in 1969 by
Twiggy.

Fringes trailed off belts, skirts and waistcoats and became associated with the hippie movement. This 1969 fringed trouser suit called 'Marisa' (left) was designed by Ossie Clark for Alice Pollock's fashionable King's Road boutique, Quorum. (Opposite) Model Kellie wears 'Tour d'Argent', a 1967 green Giselle silk Grecian dress, also by Clark. He was known for glamorous, fluid dresses such as this one.

The 1977 Christian Dior ready-to-wear collection is shown in Paris. Marc Bohan, now the chief designer at the house of Dior, is particularly remembered for his 1966 collection which was influenced by the film *Doctor Zhivago*. By 1977 shirts were no longer worn full-length, and blouson-style jackets and smock-style tops with wide sleeves had come into fashion.

A quilted wrap coat designed by Jules-François Crahay for Lanvin for autumn/winter 1977. The small, repetitive prints on the quilt juxtapose two Seventies trends: Eastern prints and fabric and the Victorian, Laura Ashley-style small-sprigged motifs. The Afghan-style scarf wrapped around the head borrows from the East.

Yves Saint Laurent outside his Rive Gauche shop in September 1969
with model Betty Calroux and muse Loulou de la Falaise. All three wear
safari-style clothes that have since become Yves Saint Laurent classics.
He launched his safari jacket in 1968, the same year that saw the
appearance of his see-through evening shirts.

The safari look went mainstream, and designers and manufacturers started to use large pockets on shirts and dresses. This button-up wool outfit by Dejac from 1973 is not advertised as a dress, but rather as a versatile coat. The shoes with their animal-skin markings complete the jungle look.

All-in-one jumpsuits and trousersuits were flung into fashion in the Seventies. This 1973 outfit revives the wide beach pyjamas and shoulders of the 1930s and is designed by Fernand Ledoux.

The coffee-coloured knickerbockers and peplum bib top were designed in 1973 by John Bates for Jean Varon, the company he helped to set up in 1964. Bates was the renowned designer of the provocative catsuits and costumes worn by Diana Rigg in the popular British television series *The Avengers*.

A three-piece suit by Yves Saint Laurent in pin-striped cloth, 1967. For evening wear Yves Saint Laurent created a woman's version of the dinner-jacket, which became known internationally as *Le Smoking*. The cut is streamlined to flatter the feminine silhouette. *Le Smoking* is still offered in Saint Laurent collections today.

Twiggy wears a looser masculine suit at London Airport, Christmas 1967. Ralph Lauren's costumes for the film *Annie Hall* (1977) reintroduced women to the notion of wearing mannish suits and borrowing clothes designed to be worn by men.

Jackie Onassis goes for the Saint Laurent and Geoffrey Beene styles in 1970 with her safari-style coat jacket and matching hipster flared trousers. By now, polo necks were unisex and were worn by everyone, just like jeans.

Brigitte Bardot goes shopping in the Via Margutta, Rome, in 1967. Trouser suits were now completely acceptable for both formal and informal occasions. In Britain, Foale & Tuffin designed sleek trouser suits such as this one.

Ursula Andress leaves a shop in Ganton Street, off Carnaby Street in London, where Foale & Tuffin had their shop. Tunic-shirt trouser suits were a more relaxed version of the jacket and trouser suit, and consisted of an open-neck shirt that had to be slipped over the head and matching trousers. The style was popular as summer- and holidaywear.

A grey astrakhan shorts suit from 1971 is by Castillo. Yves Saint Laurent had brought velvet knickerbockers back into fashion, and this outfit pays homage to his style. Opaque tights and tight, black tops with close-fitting hoods gave the effect of a leotard, a fashion that would take off later in the Seventies with the disco trend.

Marsha Hunt poses in leather shorts and unisex waistcoat in 1972. Wide sleeves held in at the wrist with a cuff continued to be popular until the late Seventies. Hunt was an early member of the cast of the legendary musical *Hair*, a hippie vehicle that offered audiences a canned stage version of early Seventies youth culture.

This cool, white, linen safari suit of 1973 has a blue linen belt and matching buttons. It is designed by new sportswear house Knap. In true Seventies style the trousers sweep to a wide flare. The safari trend influenced both men's and women's clothing, and the patch pockets helped to add a modern edge to a plain trouser suit.

A skinny-rib jumper with matching knee breeches by Shar Cleod for 1970. Knits were cut tight and smooth for men and women, and polo necks, ribbed and plain, were worn with both suits and jeans. Trousers were worn tucked into boots, Cossack-style, and knicker-bockers were an important trend for day and evening.

Boots and shoes came in many guises. (Above, clockwise, from top left) Platform clogs inspired by designs such as these from 1972 were to be revived by Gucci in the 1990s; platform shoes, particularly open-toed sandals, were also favoured; novelty boots from 1970 – these bear emblems from the Beatles' *Yellow Submarine* and pin-up Betty Grable – show the enthusiasm for customisation; and funk-style snakeskin boots (from 1975) complemented the growing trend for snakeskin in clothing.

Just as white clothing was fashionable, so white boots were the smart footwear of the 1960s. These are from the 'Summer of Love', 1967. Those who did not go for the hippie look could stick a heel on their flat, white space boots for something more elegant.

These silver kid-leather sandals of 1973 (opposite) have novelty Perspex heels for posing on the dance floor. Shoes with open panels displaying the feet and a high ankle-strap were worn for day and evening at the end of the Seventies. Space *Age, Star Trek*-style boots, into which trousers could be tucked Cossack-style, were popular for both men and women. These boots from 1972 are by Pierre Cardin.

Tights were intro-
duced to women in
the 1960s as the
mini-skirt began to
render stockings
unwearable for all
but the most
provocative. By the
1970s tights were
the popular choice.
The mini-skirt put
the fashion focus
onto legs, and
opaque, printed or
brightly coloured
tights replaced the
sheer stockings of
the 1950s. These
1975 tights are
promoted as
'stockings with
built- in panties'.

A picture reminiscent of the romantic, purple-haze style promoted by Barbara Hulanicki through Biba. During the Seventies underwear was reduced to a minimum. Stretch, triangular, non-wired, second-skin bras were virtually invisible under clothing: they gave support without being obvious to the eye. This bra has a disco-style sparkle, comes with matching tights, and was probably designed for the evening.

The veiled fox fur hood and muffler (far, right) are designed by Pierre Balmain for his winter 1975 collection, contrasting the more exotic, affluent side of Seventies fashion with the small skullcaps popular at the time. Jean Patou's wide-brimmed mink hat (centre, right) was promoted to be worn for 'luxurious safaris' for autumn/winter 1972; this sporting tweed hat by Carven (above, right) was designed to be worn over a scarf or snood for autumn/winter 1974. Turbans complemented the trend for Eastern dress: this one (below, right) from 1975 is constructed from twists of astrakhan and jersey.

Celebrity hairstyles influenced the high street, too. (Above, clockwise, from top left) Joanna Lumley (another *Avengers* girl) goes for the pudding basin cut. For the truly glamorous look, women favoured long, waved tresses that framed the face with a mane of hair. Many black women gave up trying to straighten their hair and started to let it grow into more natural, Afro hairstyles, as illustrated by Marsha Hunt. Crimped hair became popular with disco babes of the Seventies.

Jerry Hall goes for the disco diva look with her long, crimped hair flicked over to one side and fluid jersey top. She and Mick Jagger joined many other celebrities at the first anniversary of legendary New York discotheque Studio 54 in the summer of 1978. For women, shiny, glossed lips and shimmering fabrics were disco favourites.

(Above, left) Sexy funk-style satin trousers like these from 1972 made use of wide, flared trouser legs to draw attention to the curvy second-skin fit at the hips and crotch. Funk style was pioneered by African-Americans during the 1970s. (Above, right) These flared, bell-bottom jeans, also from 1972 and worn in St Tropez, have a pattern of tiny embroidered stars. Jeans were now being worn by everybody. These offer a naïve, romantic look when teamed with this white Victorian-style top.

American singers the Three Degrees strike a pose on a London Street in 1974. Their dressed-up halter necks and hip-hugging jeans are much sleeker than the popular hippie look of the time. The funky Afro-style hair of the girl on the left is much more exagger-ated than the flat, long hippie tresses. Flamboyant funk style was shown to best effect in films like *Superfly* and *Shaft*, and it was predominantly taken up by young, urban black men and women.

With the late Seventies came the disco style. Many disco clothes were sexy and tight-fitting, and shimmer, stretch and shine and high-heeled sandals were evening essentials. (Above, left) Nina Ricci's autumn/winter 1979 collection included this outfit in bold fuchsia with just a hint of a shimmering sequin boob tube underneath. Expensive? It cost £550. More reasonably priced is Mary Quant's 1978 fluid boob tube dress, 'Shoe-fly-pie', available at £38.90 (above, right).

(Above, left) Marc Bohan's bold royal blue 1976 dress with gold lamé muslin for Christian Dior uses a sparkle effect that would catch the flashing lights on the dance floor. Other styles for evening included Turkish-style trousers caught with bands at the ankle and embroidered, asymmetric tunics worn over tight trousers. Jean Patou's tangerine crepe evening dress (above, right) for spring/summer 1978 helped to show off a neat figure and would highlight a rich suntan.

Yves Saint Laurent designed this evening outfit with its sheer 'cigaline' top for his autumn/winter 1968 collection. Bows (worn at the waist in satin) and black velvet (the fabric used for this skirt) were his signature styles. Saint Laurent designed practical, powerful daywear for the working woman, but for evening gave her more seductive and alluring pieces. At the time he was regarded as a modern-day Chanel who broke boundaries and gave women a new elegance.

Fluid chiffons for evening were also adopted by the house of Chanel. This 1978 outfit combines the disco-cut, drop-waisted dress with spaghetti straps and a billowing wrap. Coco had died in 1971 but Chanel continued to be known for beautiful, classic clothes. It would not, however, break the fashion mould again until 1983, when Karl Lagerfeld was taken on as design director.

Princess Lee Radziwill, sister of Jackie Onassis, arrives with Rudolf Nureyev at the New York opera in 1974. Chiffon was used to create a fluid, elegant layer for capes, ponchos and wraps to wear over evening dresses and pyjamas.

(Above, left) Jackie Onassis wears a clinging jersey dress at a New York opening in 1977. Designer Halston, whose clothes she wore, was experimenting with soft drapery and simple jersey pieces at the time. In keeping with the Thirties revival, clutch bags were often carried for evening. (Above, right) The 'Iron Lady', British Prime Minister Margaret Thatcher, softens her image by wearing a diaphanous soft jersey dress to a ball after the 1977 Conservative Party Conference in Blackpool.

Miss World beauty contestants parade in their bathing costumes in 1973. Chunky, high heels and platform shoes were popular at the time and the women in this line-up undoubtedly benefit from the extra height they give them. Hipster-cut bikini bottoms, G-string bikinis, halter neck swimming costumes with string ties and costumes inset with plastic, Olympics-style rings were all fashionable for the beach or pool.

Aristotle Onassis gets down with actress Gina Lollobrigada at a Venice Film Festival party in 1967 (right). Her long, orange crochet dress creates a fluid line for evening but is not unflattering as a streamlined, more slimming under-dress is visible underneath. (Opposite) At the same party Baroness von Thyssen (left) stands beside Capucine (centre) in a clinging resort-style trouser outfit.

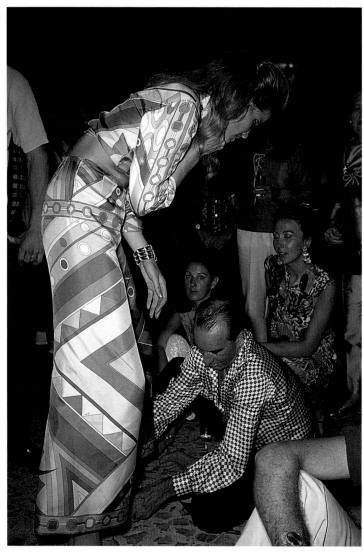

Celebrity Sixties model Veruschka wears a brightly coloured printed pyjama suit as Italian designer Emilio Pucci makes adjustments. Pucci was known for his printed silk pieces and stylish resort clothing, including capri pants, casual suits and slinky, tapered trousers. His career was launched when *Harper's Bazaar* photographed him on piste wearing ski pants he had designed himself and asked him for more of his designs. His prints were to come back into fashion for summer 2000.

Vibrant colours and prints were essentials for resortwear of the period, and this relaxed holiday outfit (above, left), perfect for pulling on after the beach, plays with a bold *trompe l'oeil* effect, 1968. (Above, right) Sexy swimming outfits with triangular cut-out panels and wrap-and-tie sections would sit somewhere between the bikini and the swimming costume. High, rope-covered wedge shoes were worn for the beach.

Just as in the Fifties, bikini tops and swimming costumes were worn with matching wraparound skirts, which meant that women could cover up elegantly if the sun became too hot and did not need to dress up to have a drink in a beach bar. All-over suntans, the darker the better, were all the rage.

G-string bikinis, which sat low on the hip and could be worn under hipster trousers, came into fashion and wide sun hats were often designed in the same fabric as a swimming costume and matching wrap sarong, 1968.

Sex symbol Farrah Fawcett, star of television series *Charlie's Angels*, relaxes in a white smock-style shirt and blue jeans (left). Blue jeans and white shirts or T-shirts provided a classless, unisex look at the time. Her long layered and blow-dried hairstyle was popular with women who aspired to Seventies glamour. Italian knitwear company Missoni, founded by husband and wife Ottavio (Tai) and Rosita Missoni, made fashionable striped and zigzag jumpers, suits, cardigan jackets and flowing dresses (opposite). Their style quickly took off because it focused on two major trends of the time: fluidity and bold patterns.

Punk set out to shock; it was a reaction against the easy-going peace and love ethic of the hippies. Women customised their clothes with safety pins, studs, razor blades and paint, and wore bold make-up. Their clothing was an eclectic mixture; it might include fetish-style leather, rubber, fishnets and cheap underwear worn as outerwear, combined with tight jeans, T-shirts, battered vests, slashed school blazers and school ties. (Opposite) Fans of punk band the Sex Pistols show off their customised T-shirts, and (right) a punk fan at a Clash concert in 1977 demonstrates punk-style DIY jewellery.

Malcom McLaren, manager of the Sex Pistols, and Vivienne Westwood, who designed and sold fetish clothing from her shop SEX on the King's Road (it later changed its name to Seditionaries). Westwood gave punks a studded and strapped bondage collection in 1976. Her bondage trousers had the legs strapped together like the underwear worn under a Poiret hobble skirt. Westwood wears the famous Sex Pistols 'God Save the Queen' T-shirt that pokes fun at the Silver Jubilee. T-shirts with pornographic images and even Nazi signs were worn by punks.

Dancers on stage with American pop group the Tubes, who toured Britain with a series of outrageous performances, most of which were banned. Their fetish and studded clothing here demonstrated the shock factor appeal of the punk movement, which young British men and women appropriated.

9 Dress to Impress

1979–1987

Japanese designer Issey Miyake's autumn/winter 1982 collection shows his almost architectural sense of design: his clothes relate to the body shape without following the body's natural lines. Miyake was one of the designers who made oversized, loose clothing popular in the Eighties, in contrast to the trend for tight Lycra pieces. His designs fuse Eastern influences from Japan with Western fashion references. In the early Eighties, Miyake brought fashion and architecture even closer together by creating clothing out of sculptural wire that stood away from the body and cast bodices of laminated polyester.

9 Dress to Impress
1979–1987

Money, money, money. Money – lots of it – was what the Eighties were all about. Margaret Thatcher and Ronald Reagan seemed to be running the world and a cut-throat consumerism had taken hold. Pat Sweeney commented in *The Face* in 1985 that the Eighties were 'making a religion of success, a cult of status, and celebrating affluence'. In fashion, logos and labels became the ultimate status symbol. 'Notice me and I'll notice you, show me your designer labels and I'll show you mine…' wrote style bible *i-D*. If you could not afford the head-to-toe designer look the accessories would do: a rucksack flashing Prada's little triangle; a gold-chained quilted bag boasting Chanel's interlinked Cs. *Drapers Record* advised in 1986: 'The height of chic is to cross the couture with the casual… wear a Chanel jacket with jeans.' Logo-splashed sportswear was at the forefront of fashion, and the style of hip-hoppers like Run DMC raised Nike and Adidas to the height of cool.

The glittering *faux opulence* of television soaps such as *Dallas* and *Dynasty* epitomised mid-Eighties glamour. Paris fashion developed the look. Karl Lagerfeld brought Chanel bang up to date with his witty take on Coco's classic style. He piled on the gold, did Chanel suits in denim and towelling and used pearls the size of ping-pong balls. 'It was just before the Stock Exchange crashed in New York, before the Gulf War, before the recession and everything was easy… there was no shame in luxury,' says Christian Lacroix. He saw a gap in the market for lavish designs for women who wanted to spend serious money, and in 1987 set up a couture house.

In the Eighties Japanese designers were hugely influential. Comme des Garçons, Yohji Yamamoto and Issey Miyake provided a fuss-free antidote to the excessive opulence of the Parisian collections. They played with sculptural wrapping and draping to make voluminous shapes in monotone colours; they pushed garment construction and fabric technology to the limits. Miyake's pleating and Comme des Garçons' purposeful knitted-in holes to create ripped effects were revolutionary. Their minimal approach helped to influence the head-to-toe black uniform of the street.

With the growth of new technology, trends began to move faster and became harder to pin down. Fashion mutated and ideas ping-ponged between the catwalk and the street. Even that punk stand-by, the Doc Marten boot, evolved: popular in the Seventies, it was raised to high-fashion status by Comme des Garçons and Yamamoto and then went back on to the street as a shoe.

The New Romantic movement, whose members bopped away at London's Blitz club in highwayman frills and long dresses, was raised to high fashion in Vivienne Westwood's 1981 Pirate collection. But who influenced whom? With their roots in the Eighties club scene, a stream of young designers including John Richmond, Body Map and Helen Storey made their names. Katharine Hamnett offered ripped jeans and T-shirts stamped with ecological slogans and Jean-Paul Gaultier put underwear over outerwear and women into power suits. Virtuoso designers such as John Galliano and Vivienne Westwood delved into history's fancy-dress box to put a modern spin on old techniques. Westwood created neo-Victorian 'mini-crinis' and Galliano revived Thirties glamour with his sleek bias-cutting.

With Margaret Thatcher, the 'Iron Lady', at the helm in Britain, power-dressing hit the boardroom. In the late Seventies the wide Marlene Dietrich-style shoulder pad was revitalised by designers such as Thierry Mugler. Giorgio Armani took up the look, offering a new suit with wide, padded shoulders and a short, tight skirt. It took American designer Donna Karan to make the look sexy: her versatile wardrobe of scarves and leotard-style 'bodies' was to be worn with wrap skirts, jackets and suits. Her coordinates could be transformed from day to evening simply by whipping off a jacket and clipping on a pair of earrings.

The idealised body shape of the era was athletic, powerful, toned. The successful woman was expected to work out. Tracksuits, grey jersey jogging and leg warmers were now seen outside the gym. American designer Norma Kamali brought women leggings and the cheer-leader's rah-rah skirt. Lycra, the super-stretch fibre, enabled designers like Azzedine Alaïa to make tight-stretch mini-skirts and tube dresses to show off the benefits of all those hours spent at the gym.

(Above, left) A neat velvet jacket and dark blue taffeta, trellis-print dress from the Christian Dior autumn/winter 1979 collection, designed by Marc Bohan. The sharp shoulders contrast with the soft, rounded skirt. Puffball skirts were coming back into fashion, for the first time (and then briefly) since the 1950s. Christian Lacroix was known for his wide, puffy, frivolous, skirts. This cocktail outfit (above, right) is by French company Kimijima for autumn/winter 1981. The silk gazar skirt is based on the petals of a flower; and the sequin boob tube sits well with the disco trend.

(Above, left) This 1980 black and white striped taffeta evening dress is also by Marc Bohan for Christian Dior. Twenties-style drop-waisted dresses were popular when they bore a short skirt, but big bows showed a return to the lavish mind-set of the *Belle Epoque*. Thick belts and sashes were fashionable accessories. The drop-waisted effect is created here (above, right) by a blouson jacket placed over a short, flared dress. Ballooning and puffed sleeves, tops and skirts had come back into fashion. They were most popular for voluminous evening designs.

Model and actress Lauren Hutton goes for the disco look at the 1980 Oscars with a fluid metallic dress. This was the more elegant edge of disco, especially when compared with skin-tight, stretch clothing. Designers used metallic, sequinned and lamé fabrics that would shimmer on the dance floor. Fluid, drop-waisted dresses with short skirts mark the look as pure Eighties.

Farah Fawcett, wearing a rah-rah skirt, bops away at a Christmas party in 1981 with newer, bigger Eighties-style hair. Norma Kamali raised the rah-rah from cheer-leader uniform to mainstream fashion. It reintroduced the mini-skirt to women after the maxi-skirts of the Seventies.

Actress Nastassja Kinski shows that short skirts were back in fashion at the beginning of the Eighties. The look is still fluid and easy. The top of the dress resembles a sweat-shirt, in line with the gym-to-the-street styles designer Norma Kamali helped to pioneer.

Imitating to flatter, Canadian fans of Boy George and Culture Club at a concert in
1984. The New Romantic style, which evolved from the punk movement,
attracted pop stars such as Adam Ant and Boy George. They took up this
historical, fancy dress style with its frilly shirts, sashes and knee breeches. Not to
be outdone, girls wore romantic dresses and bold make-up.

The man himself: Boy George on stage with Culture Club in Tokyo in summer 1984. Both Boy George and fellow pop singer Marilyn symbolised the gender-bender Eighties, when boys dressed like the girls in frills and make-up. Jean-Paul Gaultier put boys in skirts and girls wore power suits. The glam stage outfits of David Bowie and Marc Bolan in the Seventies were the precursors of this style.

Designer jeans caused a sensation when they were sold ready-ripped, and black bomber jackets were an essential part of the streetwear wardrobe. Black rucksacks, preferably by Prada, were the hot accessories. A 'fly-girl' style had emerged from New York with hip hop and break dancing and through rap groups such as Run DMC it became mainstream. Logoed trainers by Adidas, Fila and Nike and track suits, leggings and big jewellery all caught on.

Two New Romantics outside London's Blitz club in 1979. Followers of this post-punk movement strutted their stuff at Bowie Night, first held at Gossips, and then at the Blitz. The ornate, Indian-style face jewellery, softened make-up and black lace bodice show how punk's hard make-up, fetish clothing and safety-pin jewellery have been toned down for this new look.

Skinheads were born in the late Sixties, an offshoot of the more working-class side of mod culture. When punk appeared on the scene, skinheads came back out of the woodwork and added bright mohican haircuts to their donkey jackets and Doc Martens. These skinhead girls are waiting outside a disco in Hastings in the summer of 1981. Drainpipe jeans, like the ones they are wearing, were in during the early Eighties.

Bold eye make-up and spiked hair, worn with a romantic, soft-frilled lace shirt, identify this girl as a New Romantic. Dark lipstick, whitened faces and dark eyes were taken up by goths and New Romantics and scarlet lips on a pale face framed by a sharp haircut became a mainstream look.

Lady Diana Spencer marries Prince Charles on 29 July 1981. The gauche, former kindergarten assistant instantly wowed an enraptured public with her fairy-tale dress of ivory silk, with its tight bodice, voluminous skirt and long train designed by Elizabeth and David Emanuel. The dress was widely copied and fuelled the trend for full skirts and puffed sleeves for eveningwear.

This Nina Ricci suit, from her spring/summer 1982 collection, shows how sharp shoulder pads and structural tailoring had once again become popular. (Right) Large gold buttons on clothing went with the trend for big jewellery. (Above) Melanie Griffith starred with Harrison Ford in *Working Girl* in 1988, a film in which a timid secretary assumes her boss's role. Her masculine, wide-shouldered suit is similar to businesswomen's clothes designed by Calvin Klein and Donna Karan.

The 'power suit', a mini-skirted, wide-shouldered outfit, symbolised women taking control in the workplace. These curvy versions are by Christian Dior for spring/summer 1987 and are worn with typically chunky earrings. Eighties executive woman would probably have completed the look with a Rolex watch and a Filofax.

(Right) Hip young designer Anne Dupuy makes masculine pin-striped suits for women for the Jousse collection for autumn/winter 1979. Jean-Paul Gaultier played a similar game in 1985. (Above) In 1983 Annie Lennox of the Eurythmics wore her hair cropped short and gender-bender, men's style clothing.

By 1985, Diana, Princess of Wales, had firmly discarded the Sloane Ranger look and was experimenting with more daring styles such as this dress cut low at the back and accessorised with pearls for the premiere of the film *Back to the Future*. Her hair is streaked blonde and she is considerably slimmer. She particularly favoured clothes by British designers Caroline Charles and Arabella Pollen.

Diana, Princess of Wales, strides past photographers at a wedding in 1983. Her 'power dress', with its pin-stripes and wide shoulders, and her confident walk already hint at the creation of the fashion icon she would become. As her marriage broke up she became a *tour de force*, a princess who had the nerve to break rank and challenge the Royal Family on national television.

If wide shoulders were to go to the extremes of the 1930s, volume almost reached the extremes of the 1950s. This exaggerated coat from Beretta Fashion was shown on the catwalk for autumn/winter 1982. Pierre Cardin, Thierry Mugler and Claude Montana had all introduced influential designs with extremely wide shoulders at the end of the Seventies.

The trend for outsize garments that swamped the body included baggy T-shirts and sloppy knits, which could also be worn as dresses. Here French designer Sonia Rykiel borrows from the boys for a soft, wide-shouldered look for women for her spring/summer 1982 fashion show. The bow motif, which also appeared at the throat on shirts, is used as detailing.

For her Witches collection of autumn/winter 1983, Vivienne Westwood used wrinkled tubes of fabric layered over the hips so that the skirt beneath flared out. These more conservative evening dresses by Jean-Louis Scherrer for spring/summer 1987 follow a similar silhouette. The trend for wide skirts such as these began in the discos of the early Eighties, where women wore bright tutu mini-skirts as clubwear.

The swashbuckling pirate style adopted by the New Romantics, which was also put on the catwalk by Vivienne Westwood with her Pirates collection, is interpreted here by Khan Fashions for spring/summer 1982. The frilled shirts, bold sashes and short trousers here are meant to be worn by women, but male New Romantics had adopted their own version of the look.

Jamie Lee Curtis starred alongside John Travolta as an aerobics instructor in the 1985 film *Perfect*. Work out-style fashion, influenced by jogging and aerobics, now appeared on the street. Headbands, loose tracksuit pants, trainers, large T-shirts and loose sweat tops were all popular, as were super-stretch, skin-tight tops, leggings and skirts. In America executives even started wearing trainers with their power suits on their way to work.

(Above, left) Cher with her son, Elijah Blue Allman. Her easy, loose sports trousers, relaxed vest and sloppy jacket are examples of the oversized sports clothing that had assumed such popularity at the time. A twisted headband and the essential dark glasses complete the look. Bum-bags were another sporty trend: Cher has gone for a very sophisticated leather-belt version. (Above, right) Olivia Newton-John in full aerobics gear on the set of her 1981 video *Physical*. With the emphasis now on the fully-toned, superwoman body, sports fitness clothing was very much in fashion.

'I wanna live forever' went the refrain from *Fame*, the 1980 all-singing, all-dancing film about students at the New York City High School for the Performing Arts. They frequently took to the streets of New York in their dance clothes. This picture catches the kids from *Fame* in the leggings, loose tops and legwarmers that also happened to be fashionable daywear at the time.

Bad boy of fashion Jean-Paul Gaultier offers fish tail-style skirts for spring/summer 1986 (left). The tight skirts which explode in a layer of fabric at the ankle are a longer version of the earlier tutu styles. The simple knitted tube of fabric was promoted as a versatile piece of clothing. It could be worn as a boob tube, over the hair like a hood, around the neck like a scarf, as a mini-dress or as a skirt. (Right) This androgynous model wears a tight tube skirt in 1980, combining it with a loose shirt.

Japanese designers had a major influence on fashion and offered a zen antidote to the sexy status-driven looks of the Eighties. Issey Miyake (opposite, left) and Yohji Yamamoto (above, left) offer loose clothes wrapped around the body for 1986. Black polo necks were back in fashion on the street, and could be teamed with black Levi jeans and Doc Marten shoes. Yohji Yamamoto (opposite, right) uses flat lace-up shoes and black polo necks on the catwalk in 1986. (Above, right) Issey Miyake demonstrates his sculptural knits in 1987 and his unique manipulation of materials.

Karl Lagerfeld helped to turn Chanel around to make it into a strong cult label once again. Coco Chanel had originally used gold chains to weigh down the edges of her suits, and also promoted bold costume jewellery. Lagerfeld has whipped the chains off the suits to create big gold belts and necklaces in true Eighties style.

The Eighties were about excess and nothing summed up excess more than the *haute couture* shows from which a diminishing handful of wealthy women ordered expensive made-to-measure clothes. The couture collections continued predominantly as a marketing tool from which to sell ready-to-wear, cosmetics and scent. This winter outfit (above, left) for 1983 is by the house of Lanvin. Yves Saint Laurent shows an opulent dress and jacket for his autumn/winter 1982 collection (above, right). The bodice and skirt are embellished in a way that would, by the 1990s, seem over the top.

Annie Lennox in concert in 1984. Thick belts such as the one she is wearing, reminiscent of 'waspie' waist corsets, were part of the trend for underwear-as-outerwear along with bustier bra tops. Fingerless gloves were also a key Eighties accessory, particularly when executed in lace.

Madonna in concert in America in 1985. Madonna's style was widely copied. Lacy tights, mini skirts and trashy, layered clothes were accessorised with a jumble of mixed necklaces that trailed down to the waist. Wide, cropped tops with bat wing sleeves were a key trend, along with oversized knitted jumpers.

Debbie Harry and Blondie in 1980. T-shirts with slogans were popular during the 1980s and gave the wearer the opportunity to show off their logos and labels if they so chose. Katharine Hamnett had started a trend for oversized T-shirts with big political slogans when she confronted Margaret Thatcher in 1984.

Eighties-style haircuts included teased, gelled and permed, streaked peroxide glamour locks. Blonde was worn big and long with lots of body on top of the head. This style was often tied back in a 'flapper' bow, as worn by Madonna (above) in the 1980's film *Desperately Seeking Susan*. Sharp, angular bobbed hair, sometimes streaked with vivid colour cut a dash with a minimalist black uniform, and post-punk hair was coloured, shaved and spiked was influential for teenage and street fashions.

Hairstyle, clothes – everything about Diana, Princess of Wales, was copied. In New Zealand in 1984 devotees of Diana get the look. Few would be able to keep up with the changes that ensued as Diana became a fashion icon beyond compare.

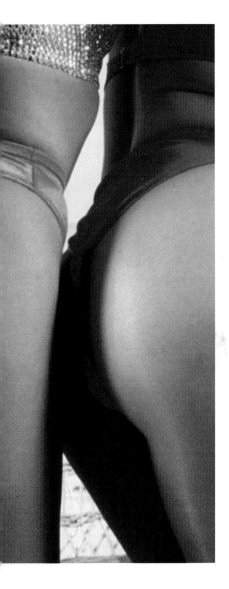

Neon for socks, tops and leggings came into fashion during the Eighties but it looked best on the beach where it gave a glow to a golden tan. Thongs ensured no (horror of horrors) 'visible panty line' under a tight mini-dress for daywear and were worn on the beach (left) for maximum tanning potential and to show off a finely toned body. These are from 1988. Neoprene, wet-suit effect material was also used for swimwear: this bustier (above) is from 1987.

Claude Montana puts his models in fur for autumn/winter 1986. He
plays with the trend for voluminous shapes and creates a top-heavy
look by combining them with tight trousers. He started out making
papier-mâché jewellery decorated with rhinestones and went on to
launch his first Claude Montana collection in 1977.

Grace Jones – in her time model, actress, singer and Bond girl – glowers at the camera in 1985. Her wide-shouldered fur coat or wrap and tube-like hood are both typical of the Eighties, as is the bold piece of jewellery worn at the throat. The anti-fur movement had garnered increasing public support. Many European women chose fake fur over real and a number of top models posed naked for an advert-isement that read 'I'd Rather Go Naked Than Wear Fur'. Not until the late 1990s did fur became more acceptable again and some of those same models wore fur on the catwalk.

On television in the Eighties soap operas came to symbolise an era of wealth and power-dressing. *Dynasty* was one such soap and it was slavishly followed. So too were the women, with their big hair, flashy jewellery, over-made-up faces and glittering, sequinned suits and opulent evening gowns. Linda Evans (left) and Joan Collins flank John Forsythe. Heather Locklear stands at the back.

Brigitte Notz, aping *Dynasty* style in real life in the Eighties, poses in Gstaad, the exclusive Swiss ski resort. Her white fur coat, all feet and tails, and her brash gold jewellery symbolise Eighties over-the-top, bad taste. Sloppy jumpers and shirts were often caught up with a fat belt worn on the hip like this one.

An Eighties model on the runway swings a Chanel bag, with its trademark gilt-chained handle. The Chanel bag became a fashion essential for those that could afford to flaunt their designer labels. It became fashionable to wear matching chain belts with Levi 501 jeans, teamed with a Chanel jacket.

Where better than Capri to show off your designer labels? Sabine Federico shows off her Chanel sweatshirt. Moschino, Chanel, Louis Vuitton (and, on the street, Nike and Adidas) were much-flaunted Eighties brands. On the high street Benetton and Naf-Naf plastered their name on sweatshirts and T-shirts. For the year 2000 logos were suddenly revived, having been virtually wiped from fashion during the Nineties.

10 Back to Basics
1988–2000

On her Blonde Ambition Tour in 1990, Madonna wore Jean-Paul Gaultier. He also used a pink-corseted, sexy torso for the shape of his scent bottle. Corsets with conical breasts to be flaunted were a Gaultier speciality, helping to promote the underwear-as-outerwear trend. The Vatican dubbed Madonna's show as 'one of the most satanic shows in the history of humanity', as a result of which she, ever the good Catholic girl, was excommunicated.

10 Back to Basics
1988–2000

'Nowadays people are looking more for what's practical; leisure time and quality of life are more important than how you dress,' explains Christian Lacroix. The theatricality of Eighties fashion gave way to New Age easy dressing. Rifat Ozbek's 1990 collection heralded the new era. It was like wiping the slate clean with hooded white tops, white trainers and crystals on strings. Big hair and shoulder pads went out of the window as the recession kicked in. Logoed clothes were consigned to the back of the wardrobe and power suits were replaced by luxury basics: cashmere T-shirts and silk pyjama pants by New York designer Zoran and the purist lines of Jil Sander.

Designers pumped more money into marketing and advertising to stimulate demand for designer labels during the recession. On the high street Gap succeeding by selling basic clothes backed by a watertight marketing strategy, and on a designer level Calvin Klein convinced the public to buy his simple cotton underwear. Muji rejected the concept of labelling its clothes altogether and sold itself as a 'non-branded' brand. While the Nineties was not about status, Gucci and Prada still managed to maintain their cachet by building up strong clothing lines which acted as marketing tools for their lucrative accessories businesses.

The end of the Nineties signalled the battle of the brands. Multinational companies were fighting for control of the major designer labels like Fendi and Gucci. One of the largest was luxury goods company LVMH Moët Hennessy Louis Vuitton. Its chairman Bernard Arnault brought in radical young British designers to pump new life into Parisian fashion. John Galliano was picked up by Givenchy and was quickly moved to Dior to make way for Alexander McQueen. He installed American Marc Jacobs at Louis Vuitton who was instrumental in lifting the brand profile with the ready-to-wear line. Their fresh approach to fashion soon made sparks fly and another luxury goods company, Richemont, put London designer Stella McCartney in place at Chloé.

At the end of the Eighties, London Fashion Week had been in trouble. 'Too many designer shows, many lacking in professionalism,' reported *Drapers Record* in 1986. Vivienne Westwood, Katharine Hamnett, John Galliano and Rifat Ozbek were no longer showing collections in London. It took a new breed of designers from Central Saint Martins College of Art and Design to kick some life into London Fashion Week. Alexander McQueen, Hussein Chalayan, Antonio Berardi and Clements Ribeiro made London the place to be. By 1995 *Drapers Record* was marvelling: 'Where else can the buyer see sophisticated eveningwear one moment and deranged models with torn black contact lenses the next? … London Fashion Week, where avant-garde and establishment rub shoulders with impunity.' Other fresh ideas were coming from Belgium and Austria: Helmut Lang's luxurious minimalism developed a cult following. Martin Margiela and Ann Demeulemeester helped to pioneer a deconstructivist aesthetic, taking minimalism one stage further.

Fashion had entered an age of pluralism. There was no single trend, but something for everybody. If anything, designers were inspired by fabric innovations and new ways of construction such as heat bonding and laser cutting. For those who wanted affordable fashion, high street multiples such as Zara, Top Shop and French Connection had never been more efficient in delivering the trends as they happened. At the end of the Nineties there was a slump. How could fashion houses persuade women to part with their cash for the latest designer jacket when they really wanted to spend it on holidays and on their homes? One way was by adding domestic products to their portfolios: you could now buy designer dog collars at Gucci and antique furniture at Nicole Farhi. Fashion products were becoming multifunctional: luxurious pashmina scarves doubled up as throws for sofas and evening handbags could pass as small decorative ornaments. Designer boutiques such as Browns in London and Colette in Paris began selling homeware and clothes under the same roof.

For autumn/winter 1999, the turn of the century, designers rejected shiny, futuristic-style clothes. Instead they chose pieces which softly wrapped the body in cream felt, boiled wool or chunky hand-knits, such as funnel-necked jackets, blanket skirts and duvet-style padded coats. Zips and buttons were hidden, almost as if they were dirty words. The body was left cocooned in ergonomic cream fabric, ready to emerge for spring 2000 in a burst of colour and print for the new century.

The build up to the second 'Summer of Love' of 1988 and the birth of rave culture started with clubs like Shoom and Project Club, parties on Ibiza, Acid House music and the drug ecstasy. Smiley face logos, loose hippie clothing, bright colours, tie dye and dungarees all became the obligatory attire. (Above) Joy parties at Shoom in 1988. (Left) The flower motif from 1967 reappears next to a smiley face for a T-shirt design. Ravers were soon congregating illegally in fields and warehouses where they would dance throughout the weekend.

Another strain of ravers came from the northern British cities such as 'Madchester', which spawned bands like the Stone Roses and the Happy Mondays. These indie ravers wore loose, slogan T-shirts and brightly coloured jeans which just got baggier and baggier. They would also travel to the weekend parties and festivals. (Right) Ravers caught by the camera in 1990.

(Left) Model Sara Stockbridge shows off a signature Vivienne Westwood corset top and platform boots. In 1990 and 1991 Westwood was awarded the prestigious British Fashion Designer of the Year Award, the first designer to win it two years in a row. During the 1990s she delved into history for inspiration for her designs, reviving platform shoes from the Seventies and going a little further back – to the 18th century – for corsets. (Above) Honor Fraser wears a mini-kilt and corset from Westwood's autumn/winter 1997 collection.

A knickerless Vivienne Westwood still had the ability to shock, even with her punk days behind her. Here she flashes for the camera at Buckingham Palace (well, why not?), where she received her OBE in December 1992. Another memorable Westwood moment came when she wore a nude-look leotard, decorated with a single green fabric fig leaf, on a television chat show.

A bare-breasted Madonna is escorted by
Jean-Paul Gaultier at the end of a fund raising
fashion show in 1992. The sailor stripes of
Gaultier's top and the pin-stripes of
Madonna's outfit were motifs that he used
again and again for his womenswear designs.

In an unconventional move, and at a time when the number of couture clients had shrunk, Jean-Paul Gaultier launched his own couture line in 1997. The move contributed to the youthful revamp of the industry, now that John Galliano and Alexander McQueen were both designing couture. This dress (above, left) is from Gaultier's first couture show and is more lavish that the typical Nineties clean-cut basics. This romantic scarf worn with a pin-striped jacket (above, right) is also from Gaultier's first couture collection of 1997. It contrasts with his 1993 collection, when he sent models onto the catwalk with tattoos and heavy piercing.

Gianni Versace was *not* known for his subtlety and minimalism. His clothes, in true Eighties style, were often excessive, loud, verging on the brash. (Above) Versace revives the Pucci tradition for silk shirts in brightly coloured prints for spring/summer 1991. Tragically, Versace was shot and killed in Miami in 1997; his sister Donatella took over as designer and head of the house.

The cult of the supermodel reached its peak in the early Nineties. A clutch of models including Naomi Campbell (British), Linda Evangelista (Canadian) and Christy Turlington (American) were raised to celebrity status in a way that only Twiggy had managed before. They demanded high fees; the media created them as personalities and followed them all over the place. Here supermodel Cindy Crawford, clad in a Gianni Versace 'bondage' gown, reports on the MTV Music Video Awards in 1992.

American actress Gwyneth Paltrow arrives at the Oscars in March 1999 with her father, director Bruce Paltrow, where she was to win the award for Best Actress for *Shakespeare in Love*. While much of Hollywood chose revealing glamour gowns for the event, Paltrow stood out in her demure pink dress, without beading or sequins, by American designer Ralph Lauren. Her acceptance speech was awash with tears.

Actress Liz Hurley
has never been
known for her
demure dresses. In
1997 she came to
public attention with
a daring slip of a
Versace dress held
together by giant
gold safety pins.
Here she arrives at
the 1998 wedding
of Henry Dent-
Brocklehurst and Lili
Maltese in another
Versace number, an
orange dress split
almost to the waist.
Even after his death,
Gianni Versace
continues to be a
popular label for
stars looking for that
show-stopping oufit.
La Hurley's bag,
incidentally, is by
Judith Leiber.

(Above, left) Princess Diana arrives at a fund raising gala in London, 1995. Her simple halter neck dress, with its plunging V-neck, is a world away from her just-married, bouffant evening frocks. She had expertly honed her personal style to a sleek, simple look. More daring eveningwear included a lace-trimmed lingerie-style dress by John Galliano, which she wore for an evening at the Metropolitan Museum of Art. In 1995 Princess Diana had also developed a more practical daywear look. She particularly favoured sharp tailoring by British designer Jasper Conran, known for his simple, flattering designs. Here (above, right) she carries a handbag with a long gold chain shoulder strap in the style of Chanel.

Princess Diana at a party in the Farnese Palace in Rome in 1996. She liked beaded dresses for the evening and was particularly fond of elegant pieces by Catherine Walker and Amanda Wakeley. Princess Diana would meet a dramatic and untimely end in a car crash, with boyfriend Dodi Fayed, in Paris in 1997.

This bold detailing from Sonia Rykiel's 1997 spring/summer collection shows her signature knitwear and stripes. Hipsters had come back into fashion at the end of the Nineties. Even tights were designed to finish on the hip, so that they could be worn under low-slung trousers such as these. Loose jersey dressing had replaced structured tailoring and was becoming more acceptable to wear in the office.

This close-up of Vivienne Westwood's collection from autumn/winter 1995 shows how she juxtaposed different styles of checks and plaids to create a clash of tartans. Westwood always emphasised the importance of garment construction and technique when designing clothes. In 1993 she moved her business on by launching her less expensive, ready-to-wear Red Label collection.

John Galliano is one of the most innovative designers of the 1990s. He was launched in 1984 when Joan Burstein, ultra-influential co-owner of London designer boutique Browns, spotted Galliano's Les Incroyables collection at his Saint Martins degree show in 1984. She bought his entire eight-piece collection, which was based on the French Revolution, and put it in her South Moulton Street shop window. This dress is from Galliano's spring/ summer 1993 collection.

Galliano presents a Union Jack jacket for spring/summer 1993. He was ever creative: he would make a dress using the same motif for his autumn/winter 1997 collection and his creations are historically researched down to the smallest detail. He offered 18th-century crinoline-style skirts for Givenchy couture spring/summer 1996, sleek Twenties dresses for autumn/winter 1994, and the neat curves and tight skirts of the 1950s for spring/summer.

In July 1997 John Galliano designed his first *haute couture* collection for Christian Dior (left), shown here, after being appointed creative director of Dior in 1996. He had originally been taken on as creative director at Givenchy in 1995, a move which was to set him up for Dior. British design talent, much of which stemmed from London's Central Saint Martins College of Art and Design, was stealthily moving in on the Paris houses.

Galliano helped to knock the stuffing out of couture by designing exquisite clothing with an edge. He paid close attention to the history of the house of Dior, giving the classic shapes a modern twist. This curvaceous couture jacket follows the lines of an original New Look Dior jacket, such as the one worn with the famous Bar suit. He also reintroduced leopard print clothing, a Dior favourite, with sexy leopard slip dresses.

John Galliano is renowned for his bias-cut slip dresses and for this reason is compared with Madame Madeleine Vionnet. In this photograph (above), two models wear bias-cut dresses in deep maroon for his autumn/winter 1999 collection. The dresses have subtle twisted detailing at the hip for a new take on the classic Galliano dress. (Opposite) Galliano prepares for his spring/summer 1997 *haute couture* show, his first for Dior.

Alexander McQueen is one of the designers who helped to revitalise London Fashion Week, raising British fashion to the height of cool. A cutting genius, his designs are often trend-setters. (Above) This theatrical skirt made of punched-out metal is worn at his 1999 show where models walked on a catwalk of frozen ice set inside glass.

In 1996 Alexander McQueen replaced John Galliano as head designer at the house of Givenchy, where he designed both the Givenchy couture and ready-to-wear lines. This sci-fi gold corseted bodice offers a supernatural look for his first Givenchy couture collection for spring/summer 1997. The theme of Greek mythology was the inspiration behind the clothing line. (Opposite, right) McQueen's Givenchy couture suit for spring/-summer 1998 demonstrates his razor-sharp tailoring skills.

Alexander McQueen is applauded after the success of his first *haute couture* collection for Givenchy in 1997. He trained at Central Saint Martins College of Art and Design and started his own label in 1993. McQueen is renowned for his 'bumster' trousers, with their revealingly low waistbands.

British model Stella Tennant (left) wears a white sailor-style trouser suit for Givenchy couture in 1997. White was an important colour for fashion in the 1990s. At the beginning of the decade it signified a fresh start after the opulence of the Eighties. During the mid-Nineties head-to-toe black was no longer fashionable.

Geri 'Ginger Spice' Halliwell, on stage at the Brit Awards in 1997 wearing a suitably patriotic but somewhat revealing dress. The Spice Girls were known for their bold, brash stage outfits and, depending on their personae, high platform boots or trainers. Their style influenced sartorially aware pre-pubescent girls and six-year-old wannabes. When Geri left the Spice Girls in 1998 she toned down her theatrical look for a more subtle, grown-up style.

Italian designers Dolce & Gabbana also celebrate Britain for their spring/summer 1999 collection. Towards the end of the Nineties, Britain experienced a wave of international acclaim for its good fashion, music and restaurants, just as in the Swinging Sixties. This dress, worn by Stella Tennant, signals a return to a 1980's style, with mini-skirts, studded bracelets and leopard-patterned tights. By the mid-Nineties, long or mid-length skirts were worn, but mini-skirts were out.

(Above, left) Belgian designer Dries van Noten shows a cosy, minimalist skirt and waistcoat for his autumn/winter 1999 collection in rich, spicy colours. At the turn of the century, many designers opted for a minimal, no-frills, cosy style, using boiled wool and felt. Antonio Berardi, known for his sassy leather clothing, offers a demure pink coat with matching vamp boots in pink leather (above, right). Berardi trained with John Galliano, working as his assistant for three years.

A wooden corset modelled at the Hussein Chalayan show, London, 1995. British designer Chalayan is known as a fashion purist who makes intellectual, minimal, well-cut clothing. He also designs the TSE cashmere line. Chalayan shot to fame when, for his Central Saint Martins degree show, he made a metal-covered dress that had been buried in the ground until it rusted.

(Above, left) A watered silk dressing gown coat by Paul Smith for autumn/winter 1998. Loose wrap-style, semi-tailored pieces such as this one were much more fashionable than structured coats and matching suits at the time. Paul Smith started off designing classic British menswear with a twist; when that proved successful, he moved into womenswear. The autumn/winter 2000 collections saw the return of tailoring and head-to-toe black outfits with an Eighties twist. German designer Jil Sander, whose clothes are modelled above (above, right), offers highly priced, minimal *de luxe* clothing.

Kate Moss in a dress by Martine Sitbon for spring/summer 1992. Sitbon makes elegant but edgy clothes and in 1988 she began to design for Chloé until Karl Lagerfeld returned in 1992. This photograph demonstrates the trend for the longer, looser style of dressing compared with the Eighties, with the emphasis on layering and mix-and-match separates rather than suits.

Icelandic pop singer Björk performing in Santiago, Chile, in summer 1998. Her all-white outfit is similar to the New Age styles of the beginning of the decade. Björk was an enthusiastic patron of up-and-coming fashion designers, particularly British, such as Jessica Ogden.

Courtney Love, lead singer of Hole, arrives at the 1992 MTV Music Awards Show in Los Angeles with her husband Kurt Cobain and daughter Frances Bean. Her simple, white, no-frills halter neck dress is reminiscent of the white glamour dresses of the 1930s. In true Nineties style she wears minimal jewellery. Courtney had a passion for designer clothes, particularly pieces by Versace.

Actress Demi Moore at Dolce & Gabbana's New York show in 1996. She starred in, and shaved her head for, Ridley Scott's *GI Jane*, but to no noticeable effect. This minimal, unisex style is the very antithesis of the thick, blonde tresses so popular during the mid-Eighties.

A lesbian couple take part in the annual Gay Pride march in London in 1993. Their tutu-style skirts are reminiscent of the skirts worn for clubbing at the beginning of the Eighties. They both have shaved their heads and wear round, matching John Lennon-style dark glasses.

Naomi Campbell goes to the market to shop for second-hand clothes. The thrift shop look appealed to women who wanted to be individual, particularly at a time when the high street was churning out mass-produced copies of anything trendy or fashionable. At the end of the Nineties there was a return to folksy, homespun hand embroidery and hand knits. Market shopping was also ideal for anyone interested in the Seventies retro look: the markets were stuffed with originals from the period.

Pierced tummy buttons, lips and eyebrows, and tribal-style ear-stretching had all become mainstream street fashion accessories (opposite, above left). The same went for tattoos. Thick, black Celtic motifs were the most popular (opposite, below right). Comfortable trainers were worn all year round and open-toed, slip-on Birkenstock sandals became the cool summer option (opposite, below left). In the Eighties sports logos were plastered all over clothes and the Adidas stripes running down the seams of clothing were all the rage (opposite, above right). Fleece was the new comfort fabric, and beanie hats such as this one from 1994 by Kenzo (right), became fashionable in the early Nineties.

At the end of the century a functional, versatile style evolved with pockets that could button on and off, clothes with zip on and off arm pieces and bags that were attached to scarves. There was an emphasis on clothes that could be comfortable in different climates, were good to travel in and would work for day through to evening. Here Michiko Koshino demonstrates a front strap rucksack.

Anna Sui was renowned for her Seventies-style hippie designs. For autumn/winter 1998 she borrows from different cultures around the world for this fur-trimmed dress and matching hood and muffler. Fashion had gone global, thanks to better communications and travel, and designers mixed influences from different cultures for a nomadic, one-world style.

Partying at a crystal party at a Russian ice rink in 1996, this girt demonstrates the trend for wearing underwear as outerwear. In Britain a decade earlier Vivienne Westwood had presented just such a look in her Buffalo collection. When the police cracked down on festivals and raves in Britain, the sound system collectives piled their speakers and records into vans to continue the free parties in Europe.

A global, hippie style had caught on with the party people. New Age travellers merged with ravers at parties reminiscent of the flower child festivals of the Seventies. Peruvian-style hats such as this one, Indian sarongs and beaded dreadlocks were mixed with combat trousers, trainers and beaten-up logo T-shirts. The catwalk did its own hippie version, called 'grunge', but it did not last. Women did not want to pay designer prices on thrift-look clothing.

Tunisian designer Azzedine Alaïa was the master of tight, sexy stretch clothing during the Eighties. His tight designs of jersey, wool-stretch, silk and leather included bustiers and stretch dresses which laced revealingly up the side of the body. Here he experiments with long overskirts layered over short in 1988, similar to Pierre Cardin's styles during the late Sixties as mini-skirts and maxi-skirts jostled for autonomy.

Turkish-born designer Rifat Ozbek was one of the more exciting young designers working in the late Eighties and early Nineties. He incorporated exotic Eastern detailing into his collections, shown here with this tribal headpiece, but his designs were slick, sharp and elegant. This was the designer who welcomed in the 1990s with his all-white New Age collection, which helped to introduce the 'less is more' trend for Nineties dressing.

Yohji Yamamoto's influence on fashion grew throughout the Nineties. A particularly memorable collection was based on a romantic wedding theme, where wide, frothy dresses were combined with mannish, tailored suits. This caped outfit for his autumn/winter 1999 show demonstrates the turn-of-the-century trend for cocoon-like clothing that swaddled the body in felt and soft, white boiled wool.

This outfit for autumn/winter 1999 by designer A.F. Vandevorst plays with tailoring shapes, but traps and cocoons the arms, so that the coat acts like a cape. Belgian and Austrian designers such as Martin Margiela and Helmut Lang respectively were well known for taking pieces of tailoring apart, and putting them back together in new ways for a deconstructionist style.

Japanese designer Rei Kawakubo of Comme des Garçon has an original and highly creative design vision, often anticipating mainstream trends before anyone else. She does not let her garments trace the natural body shape, but sculpts them around the body, using minimal shapes to contrast with voluminous frills and ruffles. This brightly coloured outfit is from her spring/summer 1992 collection.

Rei Kawakubo's clothes vault from minimalism in bright colours to minutely layered cotton rag dresses like soft petticoats. This richly brocaded dress (right) is layered over another underskirt in deep green. The Japanese school of designers, particularly Issey Miyake, was well known for breaking boundaries in terms of fabric innovation. This sheer dress by Yohji Yamamoto (far right) is marked out in triangles with multicoloured braid for a hand-crafted look for spring/summer 1997.

Yohji Yamamoto offers an earthy, knitted look for autumn/winter 1996. Knitwear and jersey boomed during the late 1990s as an alternative to tailoring. The fabric suited the long fluid skirts that were in fashion. This picture demonstrates the popular trend for layering. Long knitted cardigan coats were worn as an alternative to tailoring, just as they were during the 1920s.

The deconstructionist trend is demonstrated here in the autumn/winter 1996 collection from Yohji Yamamoto. A coat peels off the body and appears to be an unfinished garment. When Yamamoto showed his early Eighties Paris collections in body swathing black, people laughed at him. But he could live with it: the oversized look came into fashion, and Yamamoto subsequently proved that he could produce elegant, streamlined tailoring and dresses that would flatter the female figure.

Miuccia Prada summed up the easy, purist lines of the 1990s, opting for a sophisticated less-is-more style, but producing highly covetable pieces. This outfit for autumn/winter 2000 (above, left) shows the sophisticated, lady-like elegance that Prada brought back into fashion at the beginning of the 21st century. Gucci, on the other hand, opts for a retro sexy 'It' girl chic (above, right), which was slavishly copied by the high street every season. For autumn/winter 1999 Gucci did ruched velvet, black leather and lavish fur, and has set trends for sexy snakeskin and feather trimmed jeans.

For the 1990 transparent clothing was big news on the catwalks as fashion got floaty. The pieces were sold with flesh-coloured slips for decency, and chiffon tops became a mainstream trend. This outfit (above, left) is by Prada for spring/summer 1997. Seamed leather suits and sexy Seventies frills seemed the height of cool when they appeared on the Gucci catwalk for autumn/winter 2000 (above, right). American Tom Ford was brought in as design director to revamp the luxury leather goods house in 1993. As a result of this, Gucci became the status symbol of the decade.

With their clean lines and minimal detail these plain, white strapless dresses sum up the purist side of Nineties back-to-basics style. The white trend was almost surgical in its simplicity, with hidden fastenings and wrap ties. These autumn/winter 1997 dresses are by Calvin Klein, who, like Giorgio Armani, kept his designs toned down, wearable and discreet. Strapless bustiers or bandeau tops continued to be a trend, from corseted versions to stretch-style disco boob tubes.

Donna Karan goes for rock star style for her younger DKNY line in 1997. Supple, sleek leather remained fashionable throughout the 1990s and was used for skirts, dresses and shirts as well as jackets and shoes.

For autumn/winter 1999 Donna Karan offered sleek daywear in black leather. Skirts now sat below the knee or were mid-calf, a length which had been considered frumpy at the beginning of the decade.

Karan goes for a blanket-style wrap for her final collection of the Nineties. Many designers contrasted soft, cream blanket wool and sleek, black leather for their autumn/winter 1999 collections.

Like Tom Ford at Gucci, Stella McCartney turned the Chloé label into an aspirational brand. This collection, which was dedicated to her mother Linda McCartney, plays with the notion of childhood. Her spray paint-style T-shirts such as this one, and a version with an eagle motif, became best sellers for autumn/winter 1999.

She revisited the Seventies to recreate the fluid Chloé lines, from linen white dresses similar to Victorian underwear, to disco-toting denim with trellis lines of diamanté on cut-away panels. She understands what women want to wear, and makes commercial rather than intellectual clothes. Here she does her version of the hand-crafted look.

Claudia Schiffer models a feminine summer dress by Karl Lagerfeld who designed for the Chloé label, first during the Seventies and then again in the Nineties. (Overleaf) The weightless petal dresses shown by Issey Miyake for his autumn/winter 1999 collection do more than simply sum up his technical excellence and romantic vision; they offer a sense of calmness and purity, of wiping the slate clean at the dawn of a new century.

Index

About the pictures in this book

This book was created by The Hulton Getty Picture Collection which comprises over 300 separate collections and 18 million images. It is a part of Getty Images Inc., with over 70 million images and 30,000 hours of film. Picture sources for this book include: **Hulton Getty, Archive Photos** (archival photographs and film), **Liaison Agency** (news and reportage), **Online USA** (celebrity photography). All are part of Getty's press and editorial sales channel **www.gettysource.com**

How to buy or license a picture from this book

All non-Hulton images are credited individually below.

Picture licensing information

For information about licensing any image in this book, please phone
+ 44 (0)20 7579 5731,
fax: **44 (0)20 7266 3154** or
e-mail **chris.barwick@getty-images.com**

Online access

For information about Getty Images and for access to individual collections go to
www.hultongetty.com.
Go to **www.gettyone.com** for creative and conceptually oriented imagery and
www.gettysource.com for editorial images.

Buying a print

For details on how to purchase exhibition quality prints call The Hulton Getty Picture Gallery, phone
+ 44 (0)20 7276 4525 or e-mail
hulton.gallery@getty-images.com

Picture credits